TO BE HUMAN *NOW*

Pat

For your birthday —
<u>your</u> day! Exactly
sixty days late!

Love ya,

Nate

TO BE HUMAN *NOW*

by DAVID O. WOODYARD

THE WESTMINSTER PRESS · PHILADELPHIA

Scripture quotations from the Revised Standard Version of
the Bible are copyright, 1946 and 1952, by the Division of
Christian Education of the National Council of Churches,
and are used by permission.

Grateful acknowledgment is made to:
Random House, Inc., for lines from "For the Time Be-
ing." Copyright 1944 by W. H. Auden. Reprinted from
The Collected Poetry of W. H. Auden.
Charles Scribner's Sons, for a quotation from *Too Late
the Phalarope,* by Alan Paton.

STANDARD BOOK No. 664–24859–4

LIBRARY OF CONGRESS CATALOG CARD No. 70–78483

Published by The Westminster Press ®
Philadelphia, Pennsylvania

PRINTED IN THE UNITED STATES OF AMERICA

To
Robert J. McCracken

who in his ministry has lived and preached
the meaning of being human in our time

Preface

Paul Tillich has argued that the norm or central thrust of theology is produced as the experience of existence in the Christian community at a given time demands it.[1] This is not to imply that the norms of assorted eras may contradict or exclude one another but that the emphasis on one phase of the Christian message has superseded all others for the moment. From time to time the dominant question of existence shifts and seeks out another facet of our tradition for prominence. According to Tillich, the question arising out of experience during the Reformation was that of a merciful God and the possibility of forgiveness. The question dominating the early Greek church was that of finitude, death, and error. And the question Tillich perceived as arising out of his time was that of a new reality which could overcome the self-estrangement of existence. Thus the norm of theology slips around the "theological circle" laying claim to different dimensions of our historic faith. Accepting this analysis, I contend that the norm of our time is the burden "to be human *now*" and that the counterpart to that in the Christian tradition is the person of Jesus Christ.

Identifying and solidifying our essential humanness is the axial drive of contemporary life. The forces producing that concern are many but they certainly include the prospect of a war that would destroy civilization, the shift from the simplicity and intimacy of rural life to the complexity and distance of urban life, and those sciences which in the process of studying man's continuity with the natural order reduced him to well below "the angels." While earlier generations wrestled with the nature of man, ours is prone to press on to a more pragmatic obsession with what it would mean to be human in relation to ourselves and to one another. That concern inevitably leads the Christian community to Jesus Christ as being the revelation of our humanity.

The focus and outline for this book were forged from a portion of W. H. Auden's Christmas oratorio, *For the Time Being*.[2] Confronted by the beckoning yet foreboding star, each of the three Wise Men gives an account of why he is following it and then joins in a chorus that articulates what is common to their quest.

Star of the Nativity:
    I am that star most dreaded by the wise,
    For they are drawn against their will to me,

    . . . .

    I shall deprive [men] of their minor tasks.

The First Wise Man:
    To discover how to be truthful now
    Is the reason I follow this star.

The Second Wise Man:
    To discover how to be living now
    Is the reason I follow this star.

The Third Wise Man:
To discover how to be loving now
Is the reason I follow this star.

The Three Wise Men:
To discover how to be human now
Is the reason we follow this star.

The search for what it means to be human in our time is the quest that unifies these essays, and the claim that we find it at the point of "the divine ingression" their common theme. Along the way this necessitates examining what it means to be truthful about the Christian faith, what is required of us as a life-style in this particular age, and what the love imperative means amid our responsibilities and relationships.

The formation of one's humanity under Christ is through those persons living and dead who have brought their depths to ours. Whatever warmth or wisdom there may be to this book is a tribute to those who have shared their understanding of "the human thing" with this author. And that above all else is his family. The integrity of my father and the tenderness of my mother have left their mark if only in expectation. The loyalty of my sister has been a mainstay of our several families. The trustfulness and spontaneity of my wife have made the difference when nothing else could. Our two little daughters have been an infusion of joy redeeming even the worst of days. To be a son, a brother, a husband, and a father is the awesome matrix within which a man comes to his humanity in Christ—or forsakes it.

The skill and patience of my secretaries have done much to reduce the drudgery in producing this manuscript. Mrs.

Barbara Philipps and Mrs. Betty Apollonio struggled through the first draft. Mrs. Helen Dunfield labored over the final product. I am grateful both for their competence and their graciousness. I am indebted to my colleague David A. Gibbons for more influences than perhaps even he or I am aware of.

D. O. W.

Denison University
Granville, Ohio

Contents

PART ONE
"TO DISCOVER HOW TO BE TRUTHFUL NOW"

1

Why Hold Out for Christianity?

We need to confront forthrightly what for the Christian community may be the most contentious problem of our time. It is this: Is there any reason why we should think of ourselves as Christians rather than humanists? Why not become honest, forsake the pretense and sham, and cast our lot with those who do the human thing without religious regalia? Why hold out for Christianity? The reasons are certainly less clear than they once were and the culture less supportive of it. Some holding to their faith are too cautious or too indolent to attempt a radical alternative.

But for many the temptation to be a dropout is compelling if not irresistible. We ought to be honest about that. The reasons are revealing if not conclusive. There are more than a few bearing the Christian label with whom we would be delighted to disassociate. How they live, what they believe, and the things they think are important cause embarrassment. One has to concede that much of the Christian message comes through as a distracting anachronism. It is not easy to see what the verbiage of faith has to do with the technology and urban style of contemporary life. That the church is less than a vital force in the social order hardly

needs documentation. More often than not it whimpers on
the sidelines with a few saccharine exhortations. From the
state of Christianity there is much to be said for declaring
oneself a humanist. In our time it leaves less to be explained
away.

I

Why bother to hold out for Christianity? There is one
traditional answer which I choose to discredit. It is the
argument that there is a discrimination to be made at the
level of behavior. Many would say that you can tell a Christian by the way he acts. Hopefully you can in the sense that
his life is not a total repudiation of his convictions. But he
has no corner on the market when it comes to being responsible. When you examine the Christian and the humanist at
their best I don't know how you tell the difference. Michael
Novak writes: "We have been taught that there are great
and obvious differences between the Christian and the un-
believing humanist. In our actual experience it is difficult
to detect these differences. Many who call themselves
atheists or agnostics are, in the way they live and according
to the values their lives affirm, indistinguishable from
Christians. I am not trying to suggest that such people are
'hidden Christians' or 'Christians in disguise,' but on the
contrary good Christians may be nothing more than good
human beings in disguise."[3] Both at its best and at its worst
their behavior is interchangeable.

Striking confirmation of that is the extent to which Christians and humanists have made common cause with one
another on social issues. In protests against the war in Vietnam, Yale Chaplain William Coffin was surrounded and
supported by many who would not enter a church. One of

my colleagues whose aversion to clergy and churches is notorious approached me last year for funds to aid in the legal defense of Coffin, a Presbyterian minister. When I chided him for his incongruous alignment he replied with no sense of embarrassment: "I think, Dave, we are committed to *doing* the same things." Even when the verbal apparatus and institutional involvements leave us a world apart, the behavior is indistinguishable. Then there are the freedom marches for civil rights where one finds a common engagement of people with uncommon positions. How would one tell which is the Christian and which the humanist? In both, one finds the same stringent moral sensitivity, the same commitment to responsible community action, the same devotion to freedom, the same passion for justice, and the same sense of urgency. I doubt that if one could unravel the motivation of each, there would be any significant differences. I cannot even argue that there is any unique insight in the possession of Christians inaccessible to other men.

In an address by the late Albert Camus some years ago at a Dominican Monastery I was struck by his refusal to identify with Christianity yet his willingness to make common cause with Christians. He made it clear that he was an unbeliever, not because the Christian truth was an illusion, but because he could not accept it. Yet he went on to call for a kind of behavior he believed essential to every man in our time: "What the world expects of Christians is that Christians should speak out loud and clear, and that they should voice their condemnation in such a way that never a doubt, never the slightest doubt, could arise in the heart of the simplest man. That they should get away from abstraction and confront the bloodstained face that history has taken on today. The grouping we need is a grouping of men

resolved to speak out clearly and to pay up personally."[4]
Notice that he called for "a grouping of men," not humanists or Christians or atheists, but "a grouping of men" who
would engage in a certain kind of action. When it comes to
doing the human thing the Christian in his behavior has no
recognizable competence. Neither, I might add, does he
have special propensity for doing less. The old bromide
about the Crusades is irrelevant.

II

Now having said that, I still choose to hang my hat with
the Christian community. Why? I assure you it is not out of
laziness: for me it would be easier to give it up than to give
in to it. There is too much struggle and pain for that. My
rationale is this: Christianity is a symbol system—admit-
tedly one of many. It is a collection of images, stories,
rituals rooted in history by which a person relates himself
to the realities of life. The Christian faith makes accessible
to us a rich tradition of symbolic material by which we can
find our place in the universe, understand ourselves in
interaction with others, and claim the highest destiny of
which we are capable. The Christian is one who is willing
to explore these powerful symbols and in turn be pene-
trated by them. They tell it as it is, they tell it as it could
be, and they confront us with ourselves until we find our
relationship to both.

Whether we are aware of it or not, we all live by some
set of symbols. By them we make our decisions, set our
values, extend our energies, establish our goals, and express
our convictions. With them we fuse our lives into some
unity of meaning and purpose. They enable us to endure
and define the span of history it is our lot to witness. Our

lives are energized by symbols, steeped in them, and expressed by them. A number of years ago I talked with the poorest little rich girl I have ever known. Her father was board chairman of a major firm. But what disturbed and ultimately destroyed his daughter was his symbol system. It permeated and perverted every dimension of their relationship. Here is part of the way she explained it: "My father has never selected a gift for me, he has always written out a check. Last Christmas it was for one hundred thousand dollars. That may sound like a lot of money but it doesn't mean anything to me. When I tried to tell him that I was having trouble at school he picked up the phone and ordered me a new car. Last summer I wanted him to understand that I wasn't happy at home and he responded by putting in a swimming pool. He has never been there when I needed a father—only his checkbook. I've gotten to the point where I no longer think of him as a human being. He's just a bloated dollar sign." That gives you some idea of what a symbol system is and what it does to us. We all have them; Christianity is one of the options.

And I choose it. The reason is this: It answers better than any other system I have found the fundamental question, "What does it mean to be human?" I am convinced that there is nothing more crucial than living in the fullness of my possibilities as a man. The ultimate moral imperative is to be fully human and to enable others to experience the fullness of their humanity. With that the humanist and I are in full accord. We strive toward justice in the social order, we affirm the dignity of each person, we believe we are responsible for our actions in history, we aspire to compassion in response to others, we are committed to that becoming of which a man is uniquely capable. But at the center of Christianity is a living, dynamic, and intriguing symbol of what it would be like for a person to be truly and fully human. It is not enough to be committed to doing the human thing; one needs a controlling image of what it would be. The problem of the humanist is to secure himself to a reliable picture of humanness. Jesus of Nazareth is the vital symbol of that fullness of humanity which we are called to improvise in our own lives. Those who choose Jesus as the center of their symbol system never fulfill the burden of becoming human but they know what it would be like if they did. Christians belong to a historical people who have all the weaknesses of other people in history but are still hung up on the picture of humanity that appeared in the first century and has haunted, fascinated, and annoyed the race ever since. Jesus is our dynamic orientation toward reality; through him we interpret and improvise the moral imperative.

From a prison cell in Nazi Germany, Dietrich Bonhoeffer wrote: "To be a Christian does not mean to be religious in any particular way, to make something of oneself (a sinner, a penitent, or a saint) on the basis of some method or other but to be a man—not a type of man, but the man Christ creates in us."[5] That last phrase is crucial —"the man Christ creates in us." If you choose him as the center of your symbol system, you put yourself in the sphere where you not only act but are acted upon. This living symbol is not passive. It goads you to your best, it haunts you at your worst; it summons you up into what you could be, it forgives what you have been; it invites you to compassion, it brings pain upon you; it bids you laugh at your own insignificance, it gives you the sense of your own importance; it calls you into the lives of the unlovable, it enables you to get along without their love; it drives you to the heart of sorrow, it puts you alongside joy as well; it enables you to hope when all about you is despair, it brings despair upon you when you hope too much. It is the only symbol I know that pictures the fullness of humanity and demands that we improvise it in every moment.

I am an uncomfortable Christian. The present state of Christianity's traditions and institutional forms induce despair. But I cannot give it up. Christianity is my symbol system; by it I relate myself to the realities of life and the life of Reality. At its center is One who claims me both for myself and for all mankind as a human being. I am a humanist, a Christian humanist. I belong with a people who in strange and mysterious ways are enabled to move toward "mature manhood, to the measure of the stature of the fulness of Christ" (Eph. 4:13). I hold out for Christianity because I behold in Jesus the human being I am intended and enabled to be.

2

The Reality of God

When a bright college senior was asked to respond with his first thought when he heard the word "God," he said, "My grandmother." Somewhat self-consciously he explained: "Well, she was one to whom the word meant something." Then he was embarrassed, for he had revealed a truth about himself. And it is the truth about many of us. Rabbi Richard Rubenstein argues that "we live in the time of the death of God."[6] It's not that he is dead but that something has happened to the divine-human encounter. Our experience of the divine presence has shriveled until we only know how to use the divine name in profanity. Few even feel "the aching void" that was the aftertaste of withdrawal. John Osborne in his play *The Entertainer* has Jean speak for him: "Here we are, we're alone in the Universe, there's no God, it just seems that it all began by something as simple as sunlight striking a piece of rock. And here we are. We've only got ourselves. Somehow we've got to make a go of it."[7] That probably overstates the case for most. We might feel more comfortable with the words of another playwright, Paddy Chayefsky: "I think there is a God, but it is all so incomprehensible that I don't know why I should bother myself about it. I think about me and those about me. There is plenty to keep us busy down here."[8] Some say there is a God, some say there isn't, and the impression grows that it doesn't make much difference. "There is plenty to keep us busy down here." "Somehow, we've got to make a go of it."

I

Now the obvious implication is that man and not God is at the center of the action. The significant question about our life in history is no longer, "What in the world is God doing?" but, "What with the world is man doing?" The cosmic drama is perceived as played out without divine direction. Last year ten California college students published a volume of essays, and their comments about religion were significant.[9] "My faith is behind me, not in front," one wrote. "I am not drawn ahead by the apron strings of heaven; . . . I've made no contact with God; . . . my power is in me, in all of us. Life is this power." In the same vein another professed, "The only one left to believe in is Man, so I figure we've got to prepare him for the responsibilities of being God."

Some are shocked by that; there is a dimension of arrogance of which we ought to be wary. Yet it is consonant with a prevailing stream of contemporary theology. Dietrich Bonhoeffer wrote twenty-five years ago that the world has "come of age." He meant that man has reached a maturity in which he can make do on his own; he no longer has need of a god-hypothesis to cope with himself or his environment. Modern man is not disposed to invoke a deity to do for him what he can do for himself. There is a conviction in more than a few that the possibilities are within and

between themselves for dealing with the events and even-
tualities of existence; that in fact they can make a go of
existence without "dial a deity" for intervention. This,
argues Bonhoeffer, is the meaning of the cross. God allows
himself to be edged out of the world leaving man responsible. He relates to us now at the point of our strength and
maturity, not our weakness and dependency. He has picked
us up off our knees and bids us stand tall. At last the old
Greek concept of god has died. Thank God for that! You
remember how it was in the Greek theater, don't you?
When a tragedy got out of human proportions, or seemingly
so, a gigantic crane swept over the stage and deposited an
appropriate deity to solve the problem. For most of us that
is meaningless if not insulting. We are determined to wrestle
with life horizontally, man to man, moment to moment.
We're alone in the universe, but we're not lonely.

This is really what Archibald MacLeish was saying to us
with his play *J.B.* His modern Job along with Sarah was the
embodiment of tragedy. One of their daughters had been
raped and murdered by an idiot and another crushed to
death in a landslide. One son had been senselessly killed in
military training, and two others smeared across the high-
way by a drunken youth. In the final moments of the play
Sarah holds J.B. in her arms and says:

> Blow on the coals of the heart.
> The candles in churches are out.
> The lights have gone out in the sky.
> Blow on the coals of the heart.
> And we'll see by and by . . .[10]

Ten years ago I thought that the most pitiable scene on
Broadway. The whiff of arrogance suffused my senses. It's
there all right, but not the point. Now I see man "come of

age." Sarah and J.B. were taking radical responsibility for their lives, not looking elsewhere than to themselves and each other for resolution of their problems. When God allowed the cross, he demanded as much.

As that people whose symbol is the cross, we can embrace the challenge of preparing ourselves for the responsibility of being God. And the task has radical implications. We cannot pray the way we used to for the needs and disabilities of others—invoking divine intervention; we have to declare our own responsibility for meeting their conditions as best we can. We have to scratch from our vocabulary that chilling phrase, "God willing," as an expectation of benevolence; whether or not the right action comes about is a function of our initiative and inventiveness. The expectation that God will rear back and pull off a miracle to reverse circumstances we dislike must be rejected; then we can choose our attitude toward whatever is and make the best of it. We can stop deceiving ourselves about a next world in which things get evened up; there is this world to be dealt with, changing what we can and accepting what we can't. We are the people under the cross who have "come of age."

There will be some who think it all sounds like atheism dressed in a tuxedo with white tie. Let them think that; we aren't accountable for our beliefs to that penurious piety which claims to have truth in its vest pocket and righteousness in its hip pocket. After all, they called the first Christians atheists. And the reason was they denied the gods popular among the masses. It will be a sign of our faith in God if we deny that supernatural entity whom men believe resides in heaven and calls the plays from off the field. There's no God like that, save as our projections have made him so. Critics of the faith jab our ribs with the old claim that God dwarfs man, stunts growth. Some concepts do. But the God of the cross bids man live without him even as we live before him. He calls us to grasp ourselves and all of history as if we were God, limited by the fact we are not.

II

But how, then, shall we speak of God? What can we say to give substance to that three-letter word which John Updike calls an "ominous hollow noun." I'm sure of one thing: not much can be said about God. Attempts to speak of who he is haven't the audibility of a whisper in a crowded subway. And it won't do any good to set the sounds on hi-fidelity. The problem is neither volume nor frequency. It's with the words themselves. But while we can say little about God, we can describe what the word designates in our lives. When I declare the reality of God, I am affirming something about existence. And what I am asserting is that it is good to be, to exist; that my life, the lives of others, our interaction, and the larger picture in which we participate is worthwhile. Existence is trustworthy. It is permeated with positive value. Life may have its ups and downs, but on balance I am led into a conviction of confidence. There is a fundamental certainty about the goodness of the human enterprise that is challenged at times but remains unshaken. In the words of Schubert Ogden, "The word 'God' . . . provides the designation for whatever it is about this experienced whole that calls forth and justifies our original and inescapable trust."[11] It is the way we symbolize and reassure ourselves that it is good to be. The function of my theism and its religious exercises is to express and celebrate the reality "of our ineradicable confidence in the final worth of our existence."[12] It's the way I voice and reclaim a positive and affirmative appraisal of being alive. God does not exist for me in heaven; he is the ground of existence on earth, what makes it real and realizable. And all the rites of faith—prayer, worship, sacraments, and the like—are means by which I am renewed and restored in this primordial confidence.

Last year a student said to me, "I'm not sure I believe in God," then added, "but I am confident there is something behind it all." There was a time I would have landed on the vagueness of that with the full burden of orthodoxy. But now I interpret it as an affirmation of God's reality. That sentence expresses a conviction about existence. It is saying that there is worth, meaning, significance to it all. To exist is not to be caught in a hostile clutch from which we cannot squirm loose; it is good, very good, to be. And that above all else is an affirmation of what I mean by God.

The late Albert Camus went out of his way not to be known as a Christian or a believer in God. We have to respect that and not baptize him into the faith as some try. Others might argue against the effort. His central theme is that existence is essentially absurd and that would exclude him from their club. Yet what he says about man is that he can resist the encroachment of the absurd. In this sense Camus was optimistic about man and his existence. Listen to the way he describes our plight and possibilities: "We are at the extremities now. At the end of this tunnel of darkness, however, there is inevitably a light, which we already divine and for which we have to fight to insure its coming. All of us, among the ruins, are preparing a renaissance beyond the limits of nihilism."[13] I read that as a way of saying life is worthwhile, it is good to be. I don't want to call Camus a theist when he prided himself on being an unbeliever. But I have to say that his optimism about existence, his rigorous affirmation of its dignity and potentiality is what I experience as reality of God.

What I have been saying here I take to be the meaning of two texts from the Old Testament. "The eternal God is your dwelling place, and underneath are the everlasting arms." (Deut. 33:27.) And then, "Weeping may tarry for the night, but joy comes with the morning." (Ps. 30:5.) That is an ancient Hebrew way of saying: "It is good to be. Life is worthwhile." And that confidence in existence is the reality of God in our lives.

3

Passionate Love for a Ghost

There are times when Christianity has no better friends than its worst enemies. They force us to recognition when the rhetoric of faith no longer connects with anything real. Bertrand Russell performs that function. It might be argued that as a stringent antagonist of Christianity he is to our century what Friedrich Nietzsche was to his. Consider his statement about the transcendent dimension.

> The center of me is always and eternally a terrible pain—a curious wild pain—a searching for something beyond what the world contains, something transfigured and infinite, the beatific vision—God— I do not find it, I do not think it is to be found—but the love of it is my life—it's like passionate love for a ghost. . . . It is the actual spring of life in me.[14]

Most of us would not accept his conclusion that the search "for something beyond what the world contains" ends in confrontation with nothing real. That there is a God we do not deny, not most of the time. But who that God is to us, what it means to believe in him, does resemble "passionate love for a ghost." The central symbol in our faith no longer connects with our experience. We make references to God along the way but have no feel for what the referent means to us.

When a symbol loses immediacy, the temptation is to discard it. That is the easy way out, at least for me. The alternative is to explore afresh what the symbol has meant experientially and see if we can reunite the two. And here I chart my course again with the words of Schubert Ogden: "If God has any function in our life at all, if he in any way makes a difference to us, is relevant to us, and has a functional significance for us, this must be because the word 'God' when properly-used serves to designate or refer to something that our experience discloses to be in some way real, relevant, functionally significant."[15] Thus our task now is to translate the word "God" experientially, to find in our ordinary experience the presence of the extraordinary.

I

First, the word "God" designates the experience of obligation we feel as human beings. Common to our posture as persons is a relentless drive to realize what is real about us. The pressure to become our possibilities is the most vital force within us. At least in our better moments we know in ourselves a monstrous fumbling toward our limits and a haunting guilt when we have stopped short of them. Man is the being who is obligated to become. The German theologian Fritz Buri interprets this phenomenon by saying that "God is the mythological expression for the unconditionedness of personal responsibility."[16] When a person declares belief in God the focus ought not be on an entity in heaven but on a response within himself. And one dimension of that is the experience of being under orders to become. The demand for "self-enactment" is a referent in our experience for the divine name. The authentic movement of existence is into being; the real stuff of our lives is not stability, it is not deterioration, it is becoming what we can become. For that we are unalterably responsible. Martin Luther once described himself as a man driven by a team of horses—and he called it the will of God. Some would not be inclined to use such conventional phraseology, but we all can identify the experience. We are driven beyond ourselves from within ourselves toward realizing what is real about us.

Dr. Sidney Jourard, a professor of psychology at the University of Florida, writes rather interestingly about what he calls "transcendent behavior." What he means by that is not something mystical and mysterious but that propensity in all of us to go beyond ourselves. Of course this does not mean that a man extends himself beyond his real being, but beyond some limit he or others hold of him. What he transcends is a concept of his boundaries. Jourard sees man as the being who overextends himself in creativity, in physical endurance, in learning, in response to adversity, in all realms of his life. Now in his analysis of the factors in transcendent behavior he makes this commentary: "Deeply religious persons report that they experience God as a Being who perpetually challenges them; and under the instigation of this challenge, they continually bring forth from themselves achievements and feats of endurance which might be impossible for persons less challenged."[17] While that statement is rather clinical and cold, it is refreshingly similar in intent to that of theologian Buri: "God is the mythological expression for the unconditionedness of personal responsibility."

Whether or not we are comfortable with the array of

phrases I have called to bear, we are conscious of the drive
to become. It is one of the most real things about us. We
know it when we have failed ourselves completely and in
the dissatisfaction with our accomplishments. We know it
when we are thrust up against a person or situation that
evokes from us a fullness of response of which we did not
know we were capable. We know it in the setting of goals
and the momentum that wells up within us to meet them.
We know it in the surge of life that meets the depths of
tragedy with a resiliency and power exceeding expectation.
In all of us there is a raw sense of personal responsibility,
of being called forth into life; experientially, that in part is
what we mean by the word "God."

II

Secondly, the divine name designates the experience of
life itself as a becoming. The setting within which our personal responsibility transpires is one that is moving out into
a future of indeterminate possibilities. The life process is
one of movement toward what has not been before. Nothing in the past is a final boundary. History is not a dead
end but an open end. The play is not repeated, it is re-
created; the plot is not prefabricated, it is improvised; the
characters are not contoured in advance, they are conceived along the way. While there is continuity to the life
story, there is flexibility and fluidity as well. Several years
ago a young minister backed his car out of the drive one
morning and then looked forward to see that he had run
over his three-year-old son. The family had the traditional
interment at the cemetery but no funeral. A few days after
the death they gave a party for the relatives and warmest
friends. When the minister was asked why and how he

could do that, he responded: "I wanted all of us to remember together—indeed to celebrate—that one moment
of tragedy does not define all moments. We have lost one
we loved but there is a wider web of love relationships in
which to participate. There is more to life than this one
death." Implicitly he was affirming that the life process is a
becoming; there are indeterminate possibilities before us.

Some theologians in our time are saying that the being of
God himself is in becoming and that history is his body.
Schubert Ogden writes that "so far from being the wholly
absolute and immutable Being. . . . God must be conceived as the eminently relative one, whose openness to
change . . . is literally boundless. . . . He never ceases to
change in his real relations of love with his whole creation."[18] God is not a finished product; he and all of life with
him is a process of becoming. And history, not heaven, is
where God becomes. You may recall that strange scene
around a burning bush where Moses believed he had encountered the God who promised to go with the people of
Israel in their journey to an unknown land. Moses asked
after God's name which had to the Hebrew mind the implication that he was a fixed and finished entity. The answer
in this mythical encounter was, "I will be what I will be"
(Ex. 3:14). In other words, "I am the becoming one, I am
in the life process moving toward fulfillment." Many of us
over the years have been perplexed and perhaps find incredible the resurrection stories in the New Testament.
That may be because of our obsession with whether or not
they happened and if so, how. But the real significance of
the resurrection symbols is in what they say about life:
there are indeterminate possibilities, nothing is final, the
future is open, there is always more to come. That's why
the young minister to whom I referred gave a party rather

than a funeral. He wanted to celebrate the becomingness of existence. And when we use the word "God" we are talking about being called into that becoming of God in history. We are making the experience of being summoned out of secure and static places and ways and being plunged into the new. To believe in God is to trust the possibilities of life and to know that what will be is more than what has been. It is to be caught up in that becoming which death can stall but never stagger. My faith in God is an acceptance of life as a coming-to-be.

III

Thirdly, the divine name has as a referent in experience the urgency of social interaction. My becoming as a person and the process of becoming in history transpire in the corporateness of life. While the dynamics is becoming, the substance is interpersonal. Man is indissolubly bound to all men; whatever is finally real about us is social in nature. As Charles Hartshorne writes: "Social interaction is *the* dynamic principle in the universe. . . . God is the name for the ultimate, all-inclusive, cosmic society, and God is to the universal society what I am to the limited society which is my body."[19] That may be more than some would want to say, but it is a way of expressing that the divine name designates the urgency of what goes on between human beings.

Certainly the most obvious thing this means is that we do our becoming up against one another. No one knows himself by himself; no one becomes himself alone. "We only possess ourselves in the lives of others. If we are deprived of our relationships, we are deprived of our reality,"[20] writes Samuel Miller. What is real about life is relationship—or the absence of it. That's the social struc- ture of reality. Many of you know that Edward Albee writes endlessly, hauntingly, and often nauseously about our need and frustration in getting in touch with one another. One of the more significant of his plays is *The Zoo Story*. In it there is a scene where the young man who lives alone in a West Side rooming house suffered so deeply for contact with some living thing that he relates how he attempted to make it with the janitor's dog. "We regard each other with a mixture of sadness and suspicion, and then we feign indifference. We walk past each other safely; we have an understanding. It's very sad, but you'll have to admit that it is an understanding. We had made many attempts at contact, and we failed."[21] Mutuality is the stuff of existence. Selfhood is not created in a closet but in a contact.

But interpersonal engagement needs to be interpreted in another context. The inextricably social nature of life is such that my own becoming is limited by that of all man- kind. The neighbor, seen and unseen, is not only my possi- bility but my responsibility. My becoming as a human being has as its burden the bringing along of others into their possibilities. Life is an intricate web, not a string between the birth and death of one man. I cannot come into my own freedom apart from the liberation of another from his bondage. I cannot separate the food my body consumes from that which another dies without. I cannot substantiate the moment of joy without taking up into it the sorrow of a neighbor. I cannot gain an education without being bound to the illiteracy of others.

It's really not as solemn as it all sounds. The glory of life is that it is lived with intense responsibility to others. The burdens are a privilege on behalf of that whole to which we all belong. Life is of a piece, not pieces; man has a body, but mankind is a body as well. And God designates the urgency we experience in social interaction.

To believe in God is more than "passionate love for a ghost." It is to allow as a referent those experiences of life we know to be most real. Then perhaps we might strain credibility to the point of saying that it is the Trinity about which I have been thinking. God the Father is experienced as the unconditionedness of personal responsibility; God the Son is experienced as the life process in becoming and its indeterminate possibilities; and God the Holy Spirit is experienced as the urgency of social interaction.

4

A Clown Is a Poet in Action

Most of us have not been exposed to an authentic clown —at least not with any frequency. The circus arena in which the clown reigned and to which he gave cohesion has folded; the sporadic representations elsewhere in our culture are plastic at best. The artistry of Emmet Kelley and Charlie Chaplin have been replaced by the banality of Flippo on television. The clowns of Picasso and Roualt, who confronted men with the tragi-comic dimensions of existence, have been overshadowed by the superficiality of comic strip characters. Cervantes' Don Quixote, whose naïve charm stroked our sophistication until it crumbled, has been obscured by the inane predicaments in Jack Lemmon movies. While another generation used the phrase "clowning around" to name behavior with comic dimensions yet with profound meaning, our generation has settled for meaningless activity as a referent.

Yet we desert the image at our peril. We always stand in need of the clown's impact upon us, and not just for amusement. Henry Miller wrote that "a clown is a poet in action."[22] I think he meant that a clown penetrates the regions of our self-awareness with messages to which our

ears are deaf. A clown's subtlety seeps in and outmaneuvers
our defensive reactions. Perhaps more than any figure in
the arts, a clown "extends the dimension of consciousness
beyond its normal limits."[23] The clown punctures the mythology of the self until we see ourselves as we really are and
get an intimation of what we could be. As such he is an
agent of liberation and a bearer of freedom.

I

To be more specific, the most obvious thing the clown
does is to dislodge the social fictions in which we all participate. He has studied disregard for the ways in which men
uphold themselves with one another and the games they
play in the process. He assaults those curious and contrived
rituals through which we assure ourselves of position in the
social order and put ourselves across. It has been said that
the clown is the "lord of disorder." That doesn't mean he is
a revolutionary who has despaired of society, or that he is
a social outcast reaping revenge. Rather, he is contemptuous of the seriousness with which we take the systems we
have created and the false security they afford. "His incon-
gruent dress is . . . chosen with laughing contempt"[24] for the
accreditation symbols we employ. The combination of a
stiff top hat and an eighteen-inch bare foot ridicules the
insignia of dignity. The clown wants us to see how funny
we are when we take our status systems and symbols too
seriously; thus he releases us, at least momentarily, from
their restrictions. At best he enables us to see ourselves
through him and to laugh at ourselves in a redeeming
way.

You may have seen the movie *A Thousand Clowns* in
which Jason Robards starred. He portrayed one of the few

authentic clown figures of which I am aware in our time. The most obvious thing about the figure is that he would not play the social game; the rules and rituals of society were not binding upon him. A man is expected to hold a regular job and pay his way for goods received, to be utterly dependable and reliable in all his personal contacts, and to do his share toward keeping the social system in order. But Robards would have none of this; all that contributed to social cohesion was a matter of indifference. His immunity to the system was rather comprehensive. For that a dominant reaction may be contempt. And yet in the process of bringing contempt upon himself he made contemptuous the structured and stylized lives we all lead. I left the theater far less secure in the social fictions that keep me going. The clothes I wear as an insignia of position suddenly appeared spurious and farcical. The motions through which I go as a professor—the briefcase bit, the airs of infallibility, the pretensions of wisdom—suddenly seemed crude, if not cruel. The rituals of my social life and the games in which I participate at parties to put myself across seemed more pretentious and nauseous than ever before. For a moment the whole web of social fictions that engulf my existence are repulsive.

Yet what is most significant is that in the process of making us aware of the games, rituals, and roles, he does not divest us of them. For while the clown exposes them for what they are, he also knows we cannot make do without them. Social fictions provide us with the means of feeling comfortable with one another; they protect us at times from the full burden of truth that is more than we can bear; they enable us to play out in a world of illusions what would be disastrous if enacted; at times they even provide us with enough meaning to keep going when existence seems meaningless. But the clown saves us from confusing the social fictions with reality.

II

Now we can expand our understanding of the clown as an agent of self-awareness with this second phenomenon: he embraces the full range of contradictions and discrepancies in his existence.

You might say that he experiences his life as "a coincidence of opposites"—he stands always at the intersection of polar forces. The clown knows himself to be both a child of light and a child of darkness; he has the courage to affirm both his demonic depths and his angelic heights. Released at least momentarily from the social fictions in which most of us are engulfed, he can take into his self-image the realization that "he is crude and mean, but also gentle and magnanimous"; he acknowledges that he is "clumsy and inept, but, simultaneously, incredibly agile and endowed with astonishing skills"; he perceives himself as "ugly and repulsive, yet not without elegance and attractive charm."[25] Perhaps most paradoxically of all, he accepts his rejection and rejects his acceptance as if they meant both everything and nothing to him. But what is of significance is that neither confidence nor despair holds full sway. When he is sad, he is very sad, and when he is jubilant, he is very jubilant; but neither mood controls his life. His emotions run the gamut, but they return. There is always a counterpoint that sends him back toward centeredness. He knows too much that is not good about himself to be arrogant, and he knows too much that is good to be despondent. The clown takes himself for what he is, the excesses of reaction notwithstanding; he lives the grandeur and the misery of man.

There is something tremendously contagious about that kind of response to oneself. Forthrightness and truthfulness are infectious. And the supreme gift of the clown to each of us is that he evokes moments in which we see ourselves with the same clarity. Ultimately the clown cuts through the mythology we build around ourselves and calls attention to us as we really are. He expands our awareness until we admit that we are loving and thoughtful yet spiteful and careless with one another; he causes us to admit that we are consumed with ambition and passion for success yet are indolent and undisciplined; he presses in upon us the realization that we are gracious and pleasant to be with yet ugly and selfish as well; he awakens us to our confidence and security only to unveil our apprehension and uncertainty; he holds up to us the duplicity in which we sustain the personhood of one and assault the dignity of another.

And it needs to be pointed up that the recognition of oneself leads not only to integrity but to laughter. When we have borne the strain of affirming the full range of our personalities, the incongruities and the contradictions can only explode in laughter. One of the more important traits we can come by is this comic sense of self—the realization that, after all, we are rather strange creatures who ought not to be taken too seriously. The clown in pressing upon us our discrepancies saves us from the canonization of self which is our downfall. He shows us to ourselves as laughable creatures who can break loose with a smile in the very moment of intensity. When one sees himself as his own best joke, there is hope.

III

The third observation about the clown is that he always holds man under the impact of his possibilities. The only things about which he is utterly cynical are the barriers and boundaries with which human beings paralyze themselves. Walking across a tightrope over the circus tent, he laughs in the jaws of death. Thumbing his nose at dignitaries and authorities, he jokes away the position of those who would tyrannize us. Failing at some intended task, he dusts himself off and moves on as if defeat were a disposable commodity. His sad face and antics notwithstanding, the clown is always a comic and never a tragic figure. The essence of tragedy is confrontation with the immutable; the essence of comedy is exposure to the sublime and ineffable. The clown is a comic figure in that he is forever presenting us with intimations of what could be; in his own testy way he pronounces the benediction upon the walls of our imprisonment. Refusing to take with full seriousness the way things are, he presses on toward what could be.

The late Samuel H. Miller of Harvard argues that in the finest sense a clown "lives by his illusions. His dreams . . . pick him up after each dismal collapse; they repair his dignity. . . . His longings have no limit; his heart is invincible. However deep the failure, or shocking the sudden storm of embarrassment, or bewildering the descent of judgment, his tenderness is inviolable. He begins over again, whatever invisible burden his heart holds. There is a world beyond him, within him, a world of inexhaustible hope, of infinite patience, of undeniable good will."[26] Only a fool would be that foolish, and only a wise man can be a fool.

The impact of the clown is to tempt us into a different kind of relationship to the circumstances in which we find ourselves, one in which we never take them too seriously. He knows that in real life we are a curious mixture of victim and victor, but he bids us master what we can—and even extend ourselves a bit beyond that. It is better to beat one's head against a brick wall than to be crushed by a crumbling empire. What matters is not what we have to accept but what we can transform. The clown invites us to overextend ourselves lest we shrivel in retraction from life. When we live our illusions, some of them come true.

You may not have seen many clowns in your time; neither have I, not authentic ones. But remember this when you do see one: he can jar loose the social fictions in which you live, setting you free to live within them; he invites you to embrace all the discrepancies and incongruities of your life, transcending them in laughter at yourself; and he sets you under the pressure of your possibilities, tempting you to live your illusions. Then give thought to this as well: Jesus was a clown and he calls us to be "fools for Christ's sake" (I Cor. 4:10).

5
Mystery and Certainty

With religious persons there is at least the possibility of two distortions: that of pious laxity which enshrines everything in mystery and that of naïve arrogance which embroiders everything with certainty. We ought to be as repelled by the one as by the other. No one can live responsibly if he chalks up to impenetrables all the gaps in his knowledge, and no one can live honestly if he postulates false hopes. Yet many sustain their faith by isolating areas of ignorance and identifying them with God; he is what cannot otherwise be explained. And others sustain their faith by reckless affirmations; they preserve indefensible certainties by calling a moratorium on critical thought.

But authentic faith has within it the polarity of mystery and certainty. It draws its vitality and integrity from the willingness to move between what it knows and what it is unable to understand.

I

Thus it has, for one thing, "a lover's quarrel" with mystery. Though it knows that for now we are limited to seeing "in a mirror dimly" (I Cor. 13:12) it has the courage to take all its doubts into its center, refusing to equate what it does not understand with the Holy. In this struggle to disentangle sheer ignorance from mystery, faith risks the discovery of distortion in its perception of ultimacy. It even courts a willing suspension of belief that truth may be claimed in purer form. Blind affirmation is not a luxury in which the Christian need indulge himself. Thus Martin Luther permitted himself to be interrogated by an inner voice that asked of his role in the Reformation: "You alone know everything? But what if you were wrong, and if you should lead all these people into error?"[27]

What Paul Tillich says of the professional theologian is as true of the authentic Christian. He "is committed *and* alienated; he is always in faith *and* in doubt. . . . Sometimes the one side prevails, sometimes the other; and he is never certain which side really prevails."[28] Whether he attacks, rejects, or embraces the Christian message at any given moment, what matters is his "lover's quarrel" with the mystery. In a real sense his only security is his uncertainty; short of that he fossilizes truth.

To some this will constitute treason of the highest order. Faith for them is absolute certainty about things absolutely certain. To struggle against the things that pertain to God is not the province of man. Yet a sensitive reading of the Bible reveals that God has set himself up for just that! Faith is always a choice. God has made himself available to man in such a way that belief is resistible. He does not reveal himself in events immediately evident as miraculous and compelling, leaving man nothing to do but to take a deep swallow and digest. Faith is both the possibility created by God and the fulfillment actualized by man. What more stark illustration of this than the event of

Christ? Those who met him did not inevitably fall to their
knees and worship. The ones who found through him a
gracious God did so by agonizing with the reality of his
existence as it bore upon theirs.

This freedom within which we doubt and deny consti-
tutes the dynamics of faith. "Ultimate negations," writes
Joseph Sittler, "generate a strange addressability by ultimate affirmations."[29] Thus J. D. Salinger in *The Catcher
in the Rye* sets Holden Caulfield in the gallery of Radio
City Music Hall watching the Rockettes dance their "pecu-
liar obeisance to the incarnation in a tinselled Christmas
routine." There he found himself, as indeed many of us
have, "lonely and honest amidst the gurgling delight of the
audience." And he says to Sally Hayes, "Good ol' Jesus
would a 'puked.' "[30] That negation set him nearer to
the meaning of the Christmas event than all the pseudo
faith about him that thought the syncopated bouncing of
legs had something to do with praising God.

There is no faith that does not include a "lover's quarrel" with mystery. That in itself is a mark of its authenticity.

II

But the other dimension to authentic faith is the recognition that some realities are impenetrable; they cannot be
reduced to a rational system. Jewish theologian Abraham
Heschel says that "mystery is an ontological category."[31]
Far from being a challenge to the mind to conquer, it is a
limit set by reality to the reach of the mind. As Joseph
Conrad writes: "No illumination can sweep all mystery out
of the world. After the departed darkness the shadows
remain."[32] It is the inescapable situation of man to come up
against that which by its nature is beyond comprehension.

"Now we see in a mirror dimly. . . . Now I know in part."
(I Cor. 13:12.)

Authentic mystery then is not a gap in our knowledge
but a category for apprehending. Those failing to recognize
this not only are deluded about the powers of their minds
but are cheated out of experiencing a dimension of reality.
The tragic flaw in the scientist is frequently that, accus-
tomed to dealing with tangible and manageable things, he
becomes immune to the significance of all else. At the end
of his scientific career Charles Darwin confessed that he
had come to the point where he could not stand with joy
before a sunset or read with meaning a poem. The capacity
to apprehend through mystery was destroyed.

And we are all his heirs in some degree. There is the
danger that we will think we have exhausted reality when
we have come to the limit of what our minds and their
devices can grasp. Not so. We can put a man under scrutiny
—measure his physique, trace the function of his organs,
chart his behavioral responses, mark the intricate workings
of his psyche—and still miss the mystery of the human
being who lives and loves. Or we can set ourselves to
exploring the universe—determine the laws upon which it
operates, measure the matter contained in it, test its actions
and reactions—and still miss the mysterious beauty of it:
the sun setting in the west, the moon shining forth on a
harvest evening, the fall leaves screaming with resplendent
colors.

And in the arena of faith the category of mystery is at
least as integral for understanding. We can and should
study the development of doctrine, the emergence of the
Biblical records, the history of the religious community,
the evolution of moral behavior. But beyond all that is still
mystery, the mystery of the God whom we can worship

but never grasp, who loves us when all we have done argues
for rejection, who establishes meaning and hope when
everything else bespeaks despair, who comes to us in a man
of Nazareth when all his stature dictates enclosure in purity
and pride. Only a faith made flexible by mystery is adequate to the times. Through the years in Africa, Albert
Schweitzer prepared men in his parish for confirmation.
After a demonic war many of them returned to thank him
for one thing: not presenting religion as something that
explains everything. It was the creation in them of respect
for mystery that saved their faith when all about them in
the trenches men lost theirs.

None of us ought shun a "lover's quarrel" with mystery;
but neither ought we fail to recognize that mystery is a category for understanding.

III

But are we left with no more than the eternal struggle
between mystery and certainty? From time to time these
polarities fuse into the posture of awe. Solemn wonder is a
way of having rapport with reality, of making ourselves
accessible to it. Awe is not a mask for ignorance; it creates
the possibility that we will see even dimly now what
another day we will see "face to face." Life stands under
far wider horizons than reason and the senses can span in
a lifetime. Yet "awe enables us to perceive intimations of
the divine, to sense in small things the beginnings of infinite
significance, to sense the ultimate in the common and the
simple; to feel in the rush of the passing the stillness of the
eternal."[33]

Though we may be "existing doubters" by nature, we
will be men of faith only to the extent that we can stand in

wonder before horizons beyond our comprehension. Awe is the waiting room within which faith has its birth. And wait we must, though not without hope, for God is behind the mystery struggling to reveal himself. He is behind nature affirming himself as Creator of the universe; he is behind the struggle for life in a hospital room accrediting himself as life sustainer; he is behind the events of the time establishing himself as Lord of history; he is behind the relationship of a man and woman forging affection into love and sustaining the bond between them; he is behind an individual agonizing for meaning and purpose in a desperate world proclaiming himself the pathway to fulfillment; and above all he is behind the event of Christ invading all of life and claiming it as his own. The great mysteries of God are unfolded in the depths where a screech of pain, a tear of sorrow, a pinge of anxiety, a molecule of courage, a smile of joy, a laugh of relief makes itself seen and heard upon the stage of life. These are the moments in which God is known.

Nietzsche said that "before one seeks for man, one must have found the lantern." The search for an understanding of ourselves in relation to the world and whatever be ultimate within it, requires finding the lantern of awe and holding it high that its beam may be cast over horizons beyond our comprehension. For now "we see in a mirror dimly," catch intimations of the eternal passing down the twisted pathways of the temporal. But we live in the assurance that one day we will see "face to face" and then "shall understand fully, even as [we] have been fully understood" (I Cor. 13:12). For now we live between mystery and certainty, with moments of awe. That is our destiny—that is our joy!

6

Your Life Is the Liturgy

The only honest thing many of us can say about our worship experiences is that they constitute the most boring and tedious hour of the week. From childhood we have had the habit of paying our respects to God at fixed times and places, but these exercises don't mean much to us anymore. It's not so bad to sing the hymns if you don't pay attention to the words; then you needn't feel duplicity for saying things you don't believe. Prayer can be a relaxing time to let your mind wander, but there is little sense of being in touch with anything real. Scripture lessons are an exercise in futility for those whose native tongue is of the twentieth century and whose mind operated within a hundred years or so of that. And the sermon is an extended inanity projected into obscurity by one who would faint at the sight of blood. The hands of the clock drag along so mercilessly slow that one is reminded of the line in Arthur Koestler's diary when he was waiting for execution in a Spanish prison: "Time crawled through this desert of uneventfulness as though lame in both feet."[34] That may be a rather severe indictment, but it corresponds with our experience in some degree.

I

I want to expand our understanding of worship through
a text from The First Letter to the Thessalonians: "Rejoice
always; pray without ceasing; in everything give thanks"
(I Thess. 5:16–18a). Most of us identify worship as what
goes on in the time and place we set aside for God. It is a
spiritual calisthenic conducted in an atmosphere of steril-
ized goodness, the effectiveness of which is measured by
how good we feel when it is over. But the words from
Thessalonians imply that worship need not be identified
exclusively with what we traditionally think of as worship.
To understand that, we need to make a general distinction
between what is happening and what is going on. What is
happening is rather obvious to any observer—it's evident
to the eye and ear. But to grasp what is going on depends
upon one's knowledge of the human story. Walk along a
street and come upon two youngsters having at each other
rather violently, and what is happening is that they are
fighting. But what is going on is another matter. They may
be brothers giving vent to a whole range of rivalries. They
may be responding to some threat to their manhood. Or
they may merely be engaged in a competitive exercise.
What is happening and what is going on are not the same.

The relevance of that distinction is this: when what is
happening appears to be worship, that may not be what
is going on; and more importantly, when what is happening does not have the appearance of worship, that may be
precisely what is going on. But how do you know, if you
aren't willing to accept the surface clues? Here is how I
read it: When I see what was going on in the life of Jesus
going on again in the lives of men, I believe that the experience is worship. And what was going on in the life of

Jesus is that persons were becoming more human. In my theology Jesus stands for those events in which men come into their fullest possibilities as human beings, in which they realize their being, in which they get a hold on their real selves. And a Christian is the one who is concerned to participate in and initiate these humanizing events. To be specific, it's a humanizing event when you get some monkey off your back and are free to maneuver without its restraint, when you are suddenly loved and forgiven by someone in an absurd kind of way, when you are encountered by another in a manner that confirms your worth and possibilities, when you begin to take upon yourself responsibility for a social order that distorts the humanness of men, when you know that you have to live on behalf of others, not just for yourself, or when you just find yourself doing the things you know you were destined for. That's the kind of thing that was going on in the interaction of Jesus with other men; and when it reoccurs in our midst, worship is not happening but it is going on.

Let me attempt to give substance to this by reference to an event in John Steinbeck's *Sweet Thursday*. Fauna runs a whorehouse. But she is a different kind of madam. With callous realism she knows that some women are only good for bedroom exercises, while others who come under her influence have nobler possibilities. Suzy is one of the latter. And Fauna goes about the transformation by setting up a date for Suzy with one of the more respected citizens of the town. She even wraps her own furs around the little tart. At the last moment Suzy is apprehensive; she hasn't had much experience with goodness. Self-consciously she turns to the madam and asks, "Is there anything I can do for you, Fauna?" Without hesitation Fauna replies, "Yes, I want you should repeat after me, 'I'm Suzy and nobody else.' " A bit docile and perplexed she repeats, "I'm Suzy and nobody else." Fauna goes on, and "I'm a good thing." With more assurance Suzy says, "I'm a good thing." Then Fauna invites her to say, "There ain't nothing like me in the whole world." Suzy: "There ain't nothing . . ."[35] She breaks down and cries, but the tears are the joy and pain of being loved. What was happening was a conversation between a madam and one of her whores. But what was going on was the reconstitution of a person in her humanity. It's what Paul meant by the new creation in Christ. Between Fauna and Suzy in the parlor of a house of prostitution the Christ event was going on again. And I can only understand a humanizing action of that depth and intensity as worship.

II

Perhaps we can expand the point if we examine the act of prayer. We all think we know what that is. It's the time we take to talk with God, the time in which we disengage ourselves from worldly concerns for spiritual reflection. You can tell when a man is praying, because his head is bowed and his eyes are closed. If it's a minister praying in public, you can also tell by the Basil Rathbone quality of his voice. But prayer may be going on when none of these things is happening. I find the words of Bishop Robinson particularly helpful: "My own experience is that I am really praying for people, agonizing with God for them, precisely *as* I meet them and really give my soul to them. It is then if ever, in this incarnational relationship, that deep speaks to deep and the Spirit of God is able to take up our inarticulate groans and turn them into prayer."[36] You see, prayer is not turning away from others for sacred dialogue but turning toward them in a humanizing way. To pray without ceasing is not to be forever on bended knee before some absentee divine but in every moment to know that God is met, praised, and served by the extent of our humanness with one another. Prayer is not so much what we say to God but what we do on behalf of our neighbor. To participate in the struggle of the Negro for freedom is an act of intercession, to acknowledge before another our acts of inhumanity is a form of confession, to involve ourselves radically in the issues of war and peace is a form of petition, and to invite someone into the twisted regions of our loving is an invocation. I find that I am praying in any moment with another when our inhumanity is exorcised. Unconditional engagement with my neighbor in the manner of Christ is an act of worship; then if ever, I am dealing with the ground of my being.

This means that worship is more than what happens when hymns are sung, Scriptures read, and prayers offered. It's not something you can get over with on Sunday morning. Wherever you find yourself and another person is a temple, it's the most real holy ground you will ever know. Every moment is one in which you may be engaged in the humanizing action that was going on in Christ. Then there is worship—and your life is the liturgy, the most authentic liturgy ever offered to God. Perhaps when that has happened what we have traditionally perceived as worship will once again be worshipful.

PART TWO
"TO DISCOVER HOW TO BE LIVING NOW"

7

Caught on a Cloverleaf

A bright young scholar at Harvard has suggested a rather seminal image for the temper of modern life. It's like, he says, being caught on a cloverleaf.[37] Getting on and off a superhighway is a life-and-death matter. If you are in the wrong lane, it's almost impossible to exercise your intention; all about you others are moving with maximum speed and minimum control; any abrupt change of direction is apt to create a twenty-car accident; the overwhelming feeling you have is of great momentum but little maneuverability. This suggests what many of us are experiencing of life; it's like being caught on a cloverleaf.

What this means for most of us is that we have been driven from the *reflective* to the *reflexive* life. It isn't a time in which one can ponder alternatives for long. In many ways Adlai Stevenson was a symbol for that. Someone described him as the right man for the wrong time. Few have understood the age as perceptively as Stevenson, but it was said of him that he couldn't make a quick decision. What is now required of us is instant decisions, spontaneous responses to events; on the cloverleaf there are "the quick and the dead." For many in our time a shift in mood has occurred. In the 1950's a dominant concern was with self-identification. In solitude and in personal encounters persons were asking, How can I be an authentic self? They felt compelled to dissect their neuroses and seek intense relationships. There is still a place for that, but most people no longer see it as central. In the 1960's we experience the necessity of making decisions and taking action. The significant question has become, What can I do? How can I have an impact upon the pattern of history and the shape of life? We have been called outside ourselves and into a world for which we feel responsible. Thus, many are finding that the way in which we responded to life in the past is no longer relevant or effective. A new life-style is required of us. So I ask: How can we live humanly and responsibly on the cloverleaf?

I

The first thing required of us is a new style of relationships, one in which anonymity is accepted and even relished. There is a dark side to anonymity that all of us have experienced in some degree. It's fashioned in those moments in which we feel faceless in a crowd, in which we find ourselves evaporating in the sweep of events and insular relationships, in which our very personhood is vanquished. Few experiences are more threatening than that. Our traditional response has been to hunger for the encounter of self with self, to force every meeting with another into one of depth relationship. And it's followed by frustration when we fail.

But there is an alternative to fighting anonymity: it is to find a way of being human and humane in the midst of it. We can relate to others without forming a relationship; we can respond as persons while remaining nameless. Harvey Cox finds an expression of this in the parable of the good Samaritan. When the Samaritan came upon the man robbed and beaten by thieves, he did not attempt to induce an intimate encounter. He had never seen the man before and would never see him again. But in an utterly "efficient and unsentimental way"[38] he cared for the man's needs: the Samaritan bound his wounds and paid for his expenses at the inn. What the parable identifies is that we can be responsible with one another even when we are faceless to one another. Our humanness can be sustained in contacts where there is no chance or need for intimacy. And to this impersonal commerce there is a unique kind of integrity. There is none of the purchased loyalty so evident in foreign aid programs; there is not the expectation of humble gratitude which dominates the youth group's giving a turkey to a poor family at Thanksgiving; there is none of the condescension that pervades charitable activities. All that is present is "efficient and unsentimental" service to a neighbor in need.

For the most of us, anonymity is going to be an ever-increasing fact of life. We can accept it by finding ways in which we can be human and humane without emotional involvement. But we can relish it as well. Free of the need to be intimate with the multitude, we can be deeply related to the few. Being anonymous to most people permits us "to have a face and a name for others."[39] The new style of relationships, then, is one in which we are of service to the many who stand before us in need and involve ourselves with those few before whom our selfhood is nourished and expressed.

II

The second thing the cloverleaf requires of us is that we become intensely realistic about the impact we can have on our age. If there is one thing I have learned from working among college students, it is the nobility of thinking small. We need not be idealists to live by ideals. This generation is not given to dreaming elaborate dreams but to enacting modest ones. Without being visionaries who ponder endless schemes for saving the world, they set themselves to the tasks at hand. The difference between our generation and theirs is, as one sociologist explains, that the younger generation has turned all the nouns into verbs.[40] We wanted to speculate about thought, they engage in thinking; we wanted to conceptualize love, they participate in loving; we wanted to conceive ethical systems, they wrestle with ethical behavior; we wanted to ponder justice, they are concerned to be just. That doesn't mean they are all militant activists or that we were all passive. But it does mean that they are more concerned with doing what they can than with thinking what they ought. That equips them for this age in which many of us are irrelevant.

This generation's perception of how one can be responsible in the world is more modest and realistic. I doubt that they will produce any Utopian schemes. But they do ask the question: What can I do in my small way to make existence more tolerable? I suspect this is why the Peace Corps has had an appeal few of us anticipated. While it summons forth a measure of idealism, it is a conspicuously modest and functional project. No one who goes to an obscure corner of the globe to teach a farmer how to irrigate or a community how to be more hygienic can have any illusions that this will save the world from hunger or eliminate disease. But it is a way of making human life more human for someone.

It has come upon me with increasing forcefulness that this is a time in which sainthood and heroics are irrelevant, in which grandiose schemes to save the world are irrelevant. The late President Kennedy seemed to grasp that as he grew into his office. He had campaigned under the slogan "The New Frontier," with an image of the Presidency that could rectify the ills of the world. You may recall a press conference two years later in which reporters asked Mr. Kennedy how he felt about his office. "I think in the first place," he said, "that the problems are more difficult than I had imagined. Secondly, there is a limitation upon the ability of the United States to solve these problems."[41] Some read these words as disillusionment, others as hypocrisy in the light of his campaign. But they revealed him as a man for this age. The task to which he set himself and to which we are called is not the illumination of the world with an idealistic scheme, but a willingness to stand against some darkness wherever we find it. This is not a time for dreamers but for men who ask, What can I do, here, now?

III

I have been suggesting that the kind of life symbolized by the cloverleaf requires a new style of relationships, "efficient and unsentimental," and a new form of responsibility, functional and realistic. But it demands as well a new image of individualism, one that rejoices in and cultivates privacy. One of the most important capacities required by this age is the courage to be alone. This is a difficult thing about which to speak because we equate being alone with being lonely. Life sets us apart at times in ways that are painful. We take a stance at variance with the majority and are rejected; we bear a secret burden and come to believe that no one cares what happens to us; we are not accepted into a group in which we yearn to belong and therefore feel cut off from meaningful community. Then being alone is infinitely lonely.

But there is another way of being with oneself which perhaps is best expressed with the word "solitude." It suggests a solemn presence to oneself, those moments in which we find ourselves to be good company, in which we are not lonely because all that we are rises up to be with us. These can become some of the most important moments of life. They allow us to experience both the light and the dark sides of ourselves; they allow us to reflect upon our life with others, how we fulfill and disappoint them; they allow us to sort out the issues for which we will stand and those we can let pass by; they allow us to face the searching questions of why we are here and where we are going; they enable us to integrate and center our existence. It is in these moments that for some a poem is given birth, a prayer begins to form upon the lips of the heart, a dream is pondered and readies us for action. These are moments in which life begins to live again.

For many these are some of the most intensely religious experiences of life. Some years ago a philosopher said that religion is what a man does with his solitude. Many of us have scoffed at that, for it leaves so much unsaid that is essential to faith. But partial truth that it is, it doubles back on us with intensity. When in solitude a person finds solidarity with himself and begins to experience himself as a centered person, he finds himself drawn up into the divine center, lifted out of his self-centeredness into that which is more and other than himself. Some years ago a student spoke of that in a way I found compelling. We had been discussing the burdens and decisions that rested heavily upon him. Then he said this: "There is one thing which saves me from falling apart. It happens in that moment when I have crawled into bed and pulled up the covers around me. While I'm reliving the disappointments and fulfillments of the day, I find swelling up within words which I cannot speak to myself but echo from beyond: 'Be still and know that I am God' (Ps. 46:10). Then comes peace." When our privacy is lifted into the presence of the Other, we are not taken off the cloverleaf but we are no longer at its mercy.

8
The Freedom Revolution

We are living now at the crest of a freedom revolution. It began in Asia and Africa with the throwing off of colonialism. In this country it formed around Afro-Americans who asserted themselves as human beings with sit-ins and marches. Communist countries experienced it in a liberalization that undermined Stalinist austerity. University students from Berkeley to Columbia, from Japan to Turkey, from the Sorbonne to Korea have embodied it as they challenged arbitrary powers over them. There is an emerging consensus that the time has come to act against those centers of power which are unresponsive to social justice and human dignity. The freedom revolution is in the bloodstream of suffering mankind. With perhaps the most pervasive and comprehensive following of any movement in recent history, a resounding "freedom now" echoes through the corridors of the establishment. A student generation wants a piece of the action where decisions are being made that affect their destiny. Ghetto families want relief from rats which eat their children, from exploitive rents which distort their purchasing power, and from inferior merchandise which aborts their standard of living. Black youths victimized by inferior education want out of the shoeshine boy syndrome and those with adequate education want jobs equal to their training. The hungry, naked, illiterates of Appalachia have learned of the affluent society and want in on it. Their time has come, and they know it.

"Everywhere we look in the world at present," writes Eric Hoffer, "we see something trying to be born . . . a pregnant, swollen world is writhing in labor, and . . . untrained quacks are officiating as obstetricians."[42] The great danger of our time is that the freedom revolution will be possessed by those whose passion for a moment of glory will create years of disaster. The frustration created by a power structure that has maintained stability without equality, efficiency without decency, and control without compassion is accessible to opportunists as well as to men of vision and integrity. It is a quirk of history that there are times when men call for action and times when the action calls for men. We have just emerged from an era where prophetic figures stung the social fabric into awareness and discontent. Now we are in an era where the convulsions of social change call for leaders who can discipline them for a new world. We need a model for leadership in the freedom revolution and I find it in One who lost his life challenging the establishment. He was only in his twenties when he declared himself for the movement and challenged the complacency and self-righteousness of the power structure. Standing up in the synagogue, he read as his own charter words from Isaiah: "The Spirit of the Lord is upon me, because he has anointed me to preach good news to the poor. He has sent me to proclaim release to the captives and recovering of sight to the blind, to set at liberty those who are oppressed, to proclaim the acceptable year of the Lord" (Luke 4:16–19).

I

Now what strikes us first and most forcefully is the conviction that the future is the arena of a new event. The words that Jesus read bristle with the confidence that what ought to be can be and will be. They strain after the future. The man for this hour in history does not look back in anger nor around in cynicism, but ahead in expectancy. And he drives his energies relentlessly toward that vision in which the disappointments and disasters of the moment are overcome. One is reminded of that line from George Bernard Shaw, which was a favorite of Robert Kennedy's: "Some men see things as they are and say why. I dream things that never were and say why not."

Perhaps it needs to be made clear that this trust in the future is neither idealism nor optimism. Idealism in the popular sense is wishful thinking about a future that deep down one knows will never be. It's a futuristic fairy tale, fun to think about, but unreal. One frequently hears reference to "the idealism of youth," a fancifulness about the future that one outgrows with maturity. Of late the phrase has been used to explain the attraction of youth to Senator Eugene McCarthy. But it has nothing to do with idealism. His movement thrived on the conviction that there can and will be a new event in the future. When Senator McCarthy was asked after the 1968 convention what he thought he had accomplished, he said, "Well, for one thing, I have helped this generation keep hope and trust in the future." That is not idealism. Now optimism is a second cousin to idealism. It is the assumption of a happy ending. It's a *laissez-faire* version of history: leave it alone and the natural forces will work toward the best for mankind. But the one who stands in and with the freedom revolution lives beyond optimism in the conviction that the burden of becoming is his. He is a warrior with history who fights to fashion it after his vision. Neither idealistic nor optimistic, he is determined to ensure with his own life the future event in which he believes.

But what is that new event? While in every time it has a unique shape and style, at base it is a release of persons from arbitrary restraints, deprivations, and tyrannizations of their being. It is liberation from forces that prohibit their coming into their fullest possibilities. It is persons securing some control over the forces that most directly affect them. It is the sense of well-being that comes when you have been dealt with justly. In 1963 at the Washington Monument, Martin Luther King, Jr., gave expression to a particular freedom event as he saw it for his people.

> I have a dream that one day on the red hills of Georgia the sons of former slaves and the sons of former slaveowners will be able to sit down together at the table of brotherhood.
> I have a dream that one day even the State of Mississippi, a state sweltering with the heat of oppression, will be transformed into an oasis of freedom and justice. I have a dream that my four little children will one day live in a nation where they will not be judged by the color of their skin but by the content of their character. . . .
> This is our hope. This is the faith that I go back to the South with. With this faith we will be able to hew out of the mountain of despair a stone of hope.[43]

There one sees the conviction that the future is the arena of a new event—and the commitment of self to it.

II

The second dimension of the synagogue event is Jesus' self-conscious linkage with the past. He went to the synagogue (the establishment!) and read from the Scriptures (tradition!). It was to the people of power that he called for a crusade on behalf of the powerless. It was from the book of religious sentiment that he invited secular engagement. The authentic freedom event can only be tailored by those who reclaim their roots in the past; there we secure ourselves in that identity without which we flounder between opportunism and chaos.

Of course, many in our time argue that social change can only be achieved by liberating man from the guardianship of tradition and the burdens of the past. That may be true if we only examine what they have become in the present. But it is in our past and through our tradition that we find the antecedents of the freedom event after which we strain. Those who argue that we must destroy everything that is in order to establish what ought to be are suicidal. They destroy the roots of freedom. It might have been tempting for Jesus to preach overthrowal of the Temple; there would have been support for that. But he did something far more devastating. He used the past against the very people who professed to be the living embodiment of it. He employed the tradition of Israel to tell it as it is in the present. The reading from Isaiah and Jesus' commitment to its fulfillment revealed that the Jews had not cared for the poor, released the captives, or healed the sick. They were judged by their own tradition, and that is why the right-wingers, who professed to be guardians of the past, organized a lynch mob to deal with him.

You see, who we ought to be is always in the future but what we ought to be is in the past. If we divorce ourselves from it, we destroy our identity. When Dr. King spoke of his dream at the Washington Monument, these words preceded those I quoted earlier: "I have a dream that one day this nation will rise up and live out the true meaning of its creed: 'We hold these truths to be self-evident that all men are created equal.' "[44] In the service of its future he linked the nation to its past.

That not only judges the present but saves us from the parochialism into which the passion of the moment can lead us. Those whose hang-up is with the contemporary think and act on too narrow a scale. Their perspective lacks comprehensiveness and their mission becomes perverted by the fragmentariness of their vision. In the summer of 1968 I watched the Republican Convention in Miami. One theme resounded again and again—"law and order." That is something difficult to be against. Yet the theme disturbed me. I kept remembering that Dick Gregory had said that law and order is just another way of yelling "nigger." It is a respectable device for oppressing the disinherited. Then the last night of the convention Mayor John Lindsay was interviewed. When asked about law and order, he replied: "If you look back into the history of our country, you will see that law and order resulted where there was human dignity and social justice. If we attack the forces which are leading to lawlessness and disorder, our problems will abate." It was by linkage with the past that Mayor Lindsay saved an obsession with the present from parochialism.

III

I have been arguing that the freedom revolution must be led by those with the conviction that the future is the arena of a new event and a self-conscious relationship to the past. But they must also be men who can allow the two to converge on the present with an overwhelming sense of now. There must be persons who haven't the time to take their time, whose commitment to the freedom revolution is not with their lips but their lives, who are willing to pay up personally for what they believe. After Jesus had read from the Scriptures, he said, "Today this scripture has been fulfilled in your hearing" (Luke 4:21). Surely he had no illusions that, as he stood in the synagogue and read from Isaiah, the poor would be fed, the oppressed released, or the sick healed. But he was saying that the freedom revolution absorbed his whole being and he staked his life on its fulfillment. He allowed the expectations of the future and the anticipations of the past to converge on his own existence.

While some of us right now may need toning down and others tuning up, both ought to consider a parable by a Harlem minister, associate of Dr. King, and adviser to Governor Rockefeller on urban affairs:

> In the twilight years of your life, you may be sitting in some familiar easy chair . . . and your grandchildren will climb upon your lap and with enthusiasm and excitement . . . say to you: "Grandpapa, Grandmama, we had a wonderful lesson in school today. We read the historical account of how the world came to be such a wonderful place to live. We read and learned how it is now that the lion can lie down with the lamb, and every valley has been exalted, and every hill and mountain brought low, and the rough places made plain, and the crooked made straight. We read about the nonviolent movement that started in the South, and the Montgomery bus protest, and Martin Luther King, Jr., and Fred Shuttlesworth, and Ralph Abernathy, and the marches and picketing, and economic boycotts, and voter registration drives, and the fire hoses and the dogs, and the jailings, and the murders! Grandpapa, Grandmama, you were alive back in the sixties. Tell me, what did *you* do to make the world a better place in which to live?"[45]

What *are* you doing?

9

The Contemporary Obscenities

"Anything Goes—the Permissive Society." That was the feature article in the November 13, 1967, issue of *Newsweek*. If you didn't read it, the chances are you remember the cover. Off to the left was a willowy feather—held by Jane Fonda wearing nothing but a perplexed expression! It happens that I first eyed the cover in the presence of several students who scrutinized my reaction. When I blithely commented that Miss Fonda did not have an especially pretty face, the retort was, "You're really getting old!" Actually the remark was a cover-up. A person has to be careful. If you look at a picture like that too long, people may think you have a problem, and if you don't look long enough, they may think you've seen so many you have built up an immunity!

Now the argument of the article seems to be that we Americans are finding ourselves amid a startling new atmosphere in which anything is permissible. Those four-letter words which formerly defined the vocabulary of sea captains now dominate contemporary novels, and what they refer to is portrayed in a detail that leaves nothing to the imagination. In movie theaters one is exposed to portions of the anatomy that formerly were privilege of the bedroom. Even the sanctity of the nursery has been violated—one doll manufacturer has met the craze for realism by equipping the dolls with distinguishable organs. *Newsweek* concludes that we live in a time of the twilight of the taboos.

While the editors perceived themselves as reporting objectively, they were, in fact, conditioned by a rather subtle and pervasive assumption. That assumption was that an obscenity is essentially sexual, that the heart of morality hovers around the issue of to bed or not to bed. That may be the popular usage of the word, but it is not the root meaning. It is derived from the Latin *obscenus,* which means "inauspicious, ill-omened, a bad sign." An obscenity is an indication that forces are at work subverting our personhood; it is evidence that the real guts of what it means to be human are being eroded either by ideologies or by behaviors. Of course, sex can be an obscenity, but it does not exhaust the contours of the word. There are at least two contemporary obscenities far more significant and revealing. One is disengagement and the other is dispassion.

I

First, disengagement. This is the refusal to be involved in the passion and the action of one's time. The implication here is that there are two kinds of people: those who are really alive and those who are merely living. Those merely living are usually well fed, well liked, well bred, and well meaning. The painless and the pleasurable is their style of life. And much of the time we enjoy being around them. They make no demands on us. Their conversation is never disturbing. The graciousness of their lives is sup-

portive and affirming. More often than not I covet the re-
laxed existence they lead. But in reflective moments I
know that they are straw men who fear change and reject
the future, for whom mediocrity is an accomplishment and
blandness a rainbow. To their existence there is no ex-
citement, only thrills; there is no action, only motion; there
is no intensity, only duration. They are safe because they
are not alive to anything innovative, daring, or explora-
tory.

But the person who is alive is immersed in what he un-
derstands to be the passion and the action of his time. He
identifies the throb of his era and throws himself into what
he believes needs to be done with it. He aligns himself both
with an ideology and its pragmatic possibilities. Whenever
anything significant is going on, he is in the fray. When
William Coffin, the Yale chaplain, was asked why he had
given himself so radically to protesting the war in Vietnam,
his answer was at least as dramatic as he is: "Fifty years
from now when they are passing judgment upon this era
of history," he said, "I want the record to be clear that
there were at least some who stood out against this monstrous immorality." You may not agree with his assessment
of our involvement, you may not agree with the manner
of his protest, but it is difficult to impute his involvement
in the passion and the action of our time. He is at the
center of what is going on, attempting to direct it toward
goals he sees as moral.

It is obvious that the lot of most of us is less dramatic.
Yet wherever we find ourselves, there is always a unique
constellation of passion and action to embrace or reject.
Perhaps we need to be reminded that there is no such
thing as a preparation for life. There are no practice ses-
sions. In every moment and at every place, we confront

inordinate possibilities for coming alive in significant action. The issues of life and death are as near as an acquaintance who is quietly wrestling with whether or not it is worth going on. The matter of prejudice is as real as the structures in any organization of which we are a part that preclude full participation by those of a different color or creed. The potential for violence is embedded in any situation in which the channels of full communication are aborted and individuals or groups are excluded from the centers of influence. For most of us, hunger, inadequate housing, inferior education are as near as a twenty-cent bus ride to the other side of town. We need not be a multimillion-dollar federal agency to respond. A piece of the action is available to any with the sensitivity to be concerned.

Many of us would have difficulty in agreeing on what passion and action is worthy of response. But I can say without fear of contradiction that if we are not involved in what we understand it to be, we are safe but not alive. And our disengagement can only be described as an obscenity.

II

Now the second obscenity is like unto the first: it is the state of dispassion. Some years ago several very perceptive students were asked to express in a litany how they and others experienced themselves. Perhaps the most impressive line was this: "We construct our minds with steel beams and safety glass." What a magnificent way of saying that we fortify ourselves against feeling anything deeply about the lives of others. We rigidify ourselves with steel beams and protect ourselves with safety glass lest any wanton shrieks from suffering humanity interrupt our security. "But to live," the litany continued, "is to be exposed, vulnerable, to feel pain." It is to be soft inside and to have a surface easily shattered. To some men that may not sound very masculine; it doesn't fit the image some would project of ourselves. But ask a woman what manly quality she resonates with most deeply and I'll wager that more times than not she identifies that security which enables a man to reveal himself as tender on the inside.

To be a person is to react deeply to all that bends and breaks the human spirit. It is to exist in torturous sensitivity to any event in which a person's selfhood is mauled, warped, deflated, or abandoned. But the dispassionate person immunizes his feelings against what is happening to others. The crunch of a human spirit means nothing to him. Nothing ever gets to him because he looks out at the world through safety glass and is propped up by steel beams. The dispassionate person dismisses the poverty program as a handout to a bunch of oversexed bastards too lazy to work. He enjoys telling jokes that "perpetuate erroneous and slanderous stereotypes about Jews or Negroes."[46] He delights in perpetuating rumors about persons in the public eye and drops telling remarks that imply smut in others. When reminded that young men are dying by the dozens each day in Vietnam, he callously retorts, "That is war." He ridicules others because they have a "fish handshake," because they wear white socks with blue suits, or because their mannerisms do not conform with his image of masculinity. To have no compassion is an obscenity; it is a sign that our humanity is being eroded.

III

But none of us wants to recognize himself as the person who is disengaged and dispassionate. At best we think of our neighbor. But there is a text that enables me to live with the truth about myself and not to be led into despair. Even when my faith is at its lowest ebb, it is the one line the meaning of which I can live toward: "Behold, I make all things new" (Rev. 21:5). The power of renewal, the forces of restoration are the most sure thing about life I know. In the very moment I find myself disengaged, I am suddenly drawn into involvement; in the very moment of dispassion, I find myself broken open and my feelings restored. There may be nothing we can do to induce that experience of being made new. But for God's sake don't deny it when it comes. The stake is our life.

10

In but not *Of* the Middle Class

Black Power advocate Daniel Watts and urban revolutionary Saul Alinsky, and the movements they represent, have at least one thing in common: contempt for middle-class Americans. Both argue from the premise that middle-class Americans control the centers of power in our society and have geared these centers to their own benefit. But the two men differ on what needs to be done. Watts hints at extermination; Alinsky wants to manipulate them for his own purposes. Perhaps we need to be reminded that this familiar assault is upon a class to which we are intimately related. When H. Rap Brown challenges the blacks to "get whitey," he doesn't have in mind just any Caucasian. He is attacking our personal involvement in structures that have kept the Negro in slavery. When Saul Alinsky advocates revolutionary goals toward which any means are justified, it isn't an academic argument. He is registering contempt for the indifference toward the underprivileged which you and I maintain. And when the hippie forms his protest, he isn't aggressing against his mother. He is naming the entire life-style into which most of us fit so comfortably as corrupt.

Now we resent the portrait drawn of us. Yet when the

paranoia has lifted, we have to admit our vulnerability. We have not supported, much less initiated, social change because the way things are works to our advantage. Our indifference to the underprivileged has been perpetuated effortlessly by our isolation from them. And the myth of "the democratic way" has deluded us into thinking that all men have an equal chance in life. This raises a rather severe question: Can one participate in the gracious living of the middle class without being immune to the passion and action of his time? Can one live in a world of Villager dresses and Gant shirts without having one's values a carbon copy of those who do?

Recently a friend of some years made me acutely aware of the problem. He is now the president of a bank. It suddenly occurred to me as we were talking that, while I knew he was a flaming liberal Democrat, there had never been a time in which he spoke out publicly on his convictions. When I chided him he looked me coldly in the eye and said, "Back off, Dave; remember, I'm a banker and cannot afford to offend people." That made me aware once again of how difficult it is to be in but not entirely of the middle class. But it is not impossible. If it is, my whole life is a lie. I want now to suggest several ways in which many of us live in that style without embracing all the values of those who do.

I

Certainly one is that we are cynical about the ability of social systems and institutions to provide what they promise. While we cannot do without them, neither can we trust them to meet equally well the needs of all men. One of the most deeply ingrained middle-class assumptions is that the

American way of life and the democratic process guarantee
the welfare of all. That is implicit in a myriad of slogans,
most of which I was brought up on. You may have heard
them a time or two! "Anyone can make something of himself if he just has the ambition." "If the Negro wants what
I got, let him earn it." "As soon as you start helping people,
you destroy their initiative." "The great thing about the
American system is that you can go from log cabin to
White House." "Anyone with a good education can get a
good job." You may not find these maxims entirely dis-
agreeable. For years I accepted every one of them. But now
I distrust the assumption that our systems and institutions
are sound and create an environment in which anyone can
make good. That leads to incredible complacency.

When Daniel Watts visited our college town, someone
asked what ought to be done in it. Without a trace of humor
he said, "Burn it down." As a property owner I reacted
rather negatively to that project! But I didn't miss his point.
This is what he thinks it will take to make many of us
aware that the system is loaded in favor of the white man
and against the Afro-American. You probably read about
the Eartha Kitt episode at Lady Bird Johnson's luncheon
sometime ago. The majority of commentators dwelled on
her indiscretion. Mrs. Johnson regretted that the incident
obscured all the good things that were said at the affair.
The real tragedy was that the obsession with taste ob-
literated the human drama. Miss Kitt was a South Carolina
cotton picker as a child and spent her teen years in the
slums of Harlem. Even though she has made it to the top,
she knows how the system fails to protect and provide for
her people. That she had the courage, in so austere a
setting, to speak the truth as she knows it is a great moment
in American history. It was interesting to contrast state-

ments afterward by Miss Kitt and the wife of Governor
Hughes. In an attempt to explain her action the Negro
singer said, "I have to say what is in my heart." Mrs.
Hughes explained her reaction this way: "I just felt that
someone had to speak for the average American." She
might as well have said for the average middle-class American who trusts our systems absolutely. Eartha Kitt knows
better.

We transcend our environment when we recognize that
the systems and institutions of our time do not work so well
for others as they do for us.

II

Another way in which we free ourselves is by maintaining a contentious spirit. By that I mean a determination to
doubt the very things of which those around us are most
sure. Whether it gathers at the country club or at the rotary,
every group has a body of assumptions and perceptions
about which it tends to be unreflective. To draw them out
in the open is to evoke hostility, for they are the pillars
upon which our way of life rests. Implicitly we say, "Don't
confuse me with the issues, my mind is made up." But the
contentious person gravitates to these centers of consensus
and disrupts our security. He is more interested in what is
true than in what is agreed on. He knows that second-hand
values are a form of harlotry.

Anyone who reads the daily papers is aware of the extent
to which the middle class is being challenged. But it is
usually by dropouts, by those who have given up on
society. I have some reservations about that as a way of
being responsible. What is far more significant is to raise
the right questions in the wrong places—indeed, the embar-

rassing ones. I don't think much change comes about when people desert the structures but when they stand within them pecking away at their assumptions. At the university I serve, the women students proposed that self-limiting hours should replace the traditional curfew for the dorms. The motion passed the faculty with only one dissenting voice. The students' tactic was to ferret out the assumptions on which the old system rested, and these looked so bad that none of us wanted to be identified with them. Change is not always that swift or easy, but that is the way it comes about in an orderly community.

Yale Chaplain William S. Coffin has been the center of protest against the Vietnam War. What many do not know is that he comes from an affluent family and is not ashamed to share in its benefits. But he has kept himself from being brainwashed by his environment. Coffin challenges everything that is assumed and forces it into a position of defending its merits. This is precisely what he did with the draft issue. He focused upon the premise that every war in which our government becomes engaged is *ipso facto* a just war and that every able American male must take up arms. Coffin used every means at his command to undercut that assumption with the claim that a man has a right to reflect morally upon his responsibility. He is no pacifist: he fought in the Korean War and was a member of the CIA. But he cannot accept that form of patriotism which puts loyalty before morality. A contentious spirit enabled William S. Coffin to be in but not of the middle class.

III

Now there is a third technique and it is to be distrustful of what we learn about those outside our social orbit from those within it. One of the surest ways to be deceived about the way things really are is to believe what we hear from those around us. The hardest thing I have to learn from people like Daniel Watts is that I have no understanding of what the Negro is up against and what he really wants. But we all think we know and reinforce one another in our distortions. This is why Watts has given up on dialogue with the white community. I think that kind of defeatism is self-defeating. Yet I cannot argue down the claim that what we think we know is the biggest barrier to knowing anything. We trust what those who know no more than we tell us about those with whom neither of us has firsthand contact.

And the closest many of us come to testing these perceptions is to ask the Negro laundress how things are—usually when paying her at the end of the day. But she isn't going to say. The white man has taught her that it is prudent to tell him what he wants to hear. Yet, one thing has changed. There are those who are going to speak and act across the barrier. The laundress may not be leading the violence, but her friends and those she trusts are. And don't be deluded into thinking that she rejects what is going on. I asked a Negro educator how he felt about the riots in Newark, New Jersey. I was taken aback when he didn't tell me what I wanted him to. "I cannot condone violence and wanton destruction of property," he said, "but I am proud as hell of my people." Our laundress is not going to tell it as it is, and neither is our neighbor in Shaker Heights; but there are some who will, and we had better listen.

The only hope I know to avoid another civil war in this country—one in which you and I have everything to lose and the Negro nothing, because he hasn't got anything—is to expose ourselves to those outside our middle-class environment. I'm not sure how we can do that; certainly there is no one way. As a beginning we've got to distrust what those around us are telling us, and that includes the suburbanite editor of the local paper in many instances. Then some of us ought to ride the transit around parts of the city or town that mother warned against in high school. That will at least be a clue to how others live. Some ought to commit a block of time to a project dealing with urban problems. Some can arrange their location, for at least a time, outside the suburbs. I happen to have studied in New York City on the edge of Harlem. The first day I took a walk around the neighborhood (where two to three thousand live in a single block) and returned to my room and sobbed—yes, men cry, God help them when they can't! No one ever told me that human beings lived like that. It's not important how we do it; what matters is that we begin to understand persons and conditions outside our social niche.

I am convinced that it is possible to live in affluence without becoming immune to those who don't.

11

The Glory of Man

By definition a humanist is "one whose belief consists of faith in man and devotion to human well-being."[47] If that be true, God is the first humanist. No one else has ever trusted man as pervasively. Look at the record. In the creation myth God is credited with having provided the setting for the human drama but he thrust the plot into our hands. Here are the words: "And God blessed them [Adam and Eve], and God said to them, 'Be fruitful and multiply, and fill the earth and subdue it; and have dominion . . .' " (Gen. 1:28). There's a sense in which from the very beginning God resigned from the universe. Not that he washed his hands of it, but that he entrusted it to the hands of man with the demand that man glorify him in the dominionship. The confirmation of that is the cross. As Bonhoeffer suggests, there God allowed himself to be edged out of the world leaving man responsible. The conduct of human affairs is no need or desire of the Creator's. He never intended to do anything for man that man could do for himself. That above all else is faith in man and devotion to human well-being.

Now to be a human being in that frame of reference is to

enact the full prerogatives of one's being in the decisions we make. The glory of man is that he can choose himself; he is defined by his decisions. Jean-Paul Sartre says that man invents himself. That is a thrust in the right direction but it overshoots the mark. It denies the multiplicity of forces over which we have scant control. But within certain boundaries, who we are is a function of the choices we make. In every moment you and I are electing the persons we will become and absorbing the consequences of prior choices. You have no one to blame for yourself but yourself.

There are at least three decisions in which the nature of our personhood is most particularly at stake.

I

First, there is the choosing of our integrity. The root meaning of the word suggests that it is the state of being undivided; it is that quality of being which on crucial issues cannot be led into contradiction. The person of integrity has identified the points at which he will stand, notwithstanding the consequences. It is what some mean when they refer to a person as "really tough"; we may not agree with him but we respect the fundamental congruence of his life. He is predictable not because he is inflexible but because there are certain areas not open for negotiation. I suspect that there are few things for which most of us would rather be known than integrity.

But the experience many of us have of ourselves is of dividedness; we are pulled in many directions and are incapable of being decisive. I have always felt a good bit of empathy for the man whom Jesus approached and asked his name. He responded with telling insight: "My name is

Legion; for *we* are many" (Mark 5:9). Indecisiveness is probably one of the most distressing things we know about ourselves. Perhaps that is not all bad; to draw too many lines is to narrow mercilessly the boundaries of our being. Yet paradoxical as it may sound, we can choose to make our choices. We can begin to constitute ourselves as persons of integrity in the moment we take just one stand consonant with our being, defining one issue on which we will not hedge. To do that is to experience oneself as a new person and once a person has known the thrill of being undivided in one moment, one tends to settle for nothing else in others.

From a colleague in Boston, I learned of such a moment in the life of Henri Matisse, the French painter. In his younger years Matisse painted still life of a rather pedantic nature, for which there was a substantial market. Being married and the father of three children, he had an overwhelming temptation to compromise his talent. But one day he chose his own integrity. Here is the story in his own words: "I had just finished one of those pictures. It was as the previous one and very much like it. I knew that on delivery I would get the money I sorely needed. There was a temptation to deliver it, but I knew that if I yielded, it would be my artistic death. Looking back I knew that it required courage to destroy that picture, particularly since the hand of the butcher and baker were outstretched at the moment. But I did destroy it. I count my emancipation from that day."[48]

The fullness of integrity is the lot of few, if any. We are all divided in some degree and at odds with ourselves. But there can be a decisive moment for each of us—perhaps this very moment—in which we begin by one decision to constitute our integrity. We can repudiate our inauthen-

ticity and by our choice begin to liberate the full prerogatives of our being. Then we will be able to say with Matisse,
"I count my emancipation from that day."

II

The second decision is this: choosing our attitude toward
the things that happen to us. It is obvious that there are a
great many circumstances over which we have scant control. Much of the time we find ourselves at the intersection
of resolute forces we cannot rebuff. Someone we love no
longer loves us and there is nothing we can do to reverse
his feelings. Our plans for the future are postponed by the
government's foreign commitments and our chances of
objecting are nil. Death comes into the intimate circle of
love and we are helpless before its finality. It is no wonder
that through the ages men have protested that they never
asked to be born and cursed the moment of their inception.
That is our first response when life takes a wrong turn; few
of us can avoid it.

But there is another response. And it is the recognition
that in every set of circumstances we can choose our attitudes. This I have come to understand most forcefully
through the writings of Viktor Frankl, a French psychiatrist
whose philosophy was conceived in the death camps of
Auschwitz and Dachau. At one point he writes: "We who
lived in concentration camps can remember the men who
walked through the huts comforting others, giving away
their last piece of bread. They may have been few in number, but they are sufficient proof that everything can be
taken from a man but one thing: the last of the human
freedoms—to choose one's attitude in any given set of
circumstances, to choose one's own way."[49]

There are events in the lives of all of us that threaten every hope and dream we ever had. If we think otherwise, we will be disillusioned with an intensity from which we may never recover. But the possibility of choosing our attitudes toward those circumstances can never be taken from us; we only lose it by default. In the exercise of that option is our dignity as human beings and our sanity as persons. I cannot control the fact that there are people who are going to reject or mock me and the things for which I stand, but I can control whether or not I become dejected and diverted from my position. I cannot deny the fact that there are persons in positions of power with whom I disagree and who for the moment have the upper hand, but I can choose whether or not to be immobilized by the frustration or remain creative in opposition. I cannot alter those events which cancel with brutal indiscretion my hopes for the future, but I can choose whether or not to give up dreaming. I cannot deny that defeat more times than not greets my expectations and at times seems to be a way of life, but I can choose whether or not to be a defeatist.

We exercise the full range of our possibilities as human beings to the extent we decide to choose our attitudes in every circumstance. And that is another dimension of the glory of man.

III

The third decision is perhaps the most fundamental: it is the choosing of one's humanity. By that I mean the style we adopt toward one another, what our responsibility is to our neighbor. In *The Plague,* Albert Camus defined the ultimate burden of modern man—it is to be a saint without God. That has nothing to do with the cultivation of piety, but it has everything to do with the way we relate to one another in a time when divine sanctions are not the means of enforcement. It is a matter of doing right by one another for no other reason than that this is the way we appropriate our humanness.

In particular this means that we hold ourselves accountable for every action and attitude that may distort, maul, deflate, or in any way crunch the personhood of another. This does not imply that we can avoid hurting people. There are times when we cannot avoid that; there are instances when hurting is the only way of helping. If our goal in life is to avoid bringing pain, we might as well resign now; pain is part of the way things are. But there is a difference between hurting another and reducing him as a human being. I see this most clearly in relation to my children. There are many times I hurt them. The mere fact of setting a boundary that does not correspond with their desires induces anguish, to say nothing of the mood I may be in at a given time. To protect them from these sources of pain is to prepare them to live in a world that does not exist. But there are other moments in which I know I have done something quite different and that is to contract them as human beings. I have stomped on their humanness. And I can't excuse myself for those imperialistic behaviors which reduce momentarily their dignity.

Perhaps another way of saying it is that the choosing of one's humanity is the decision to be "a man for others." That has nothing to do with being an effeminate personality who has no sense of his own needs or desires. But it is a conscious decision to hold oneself responsible for maintaining the humanness of others in every situation, to affirm them in their dignity. No one can tell a person precisely what that means in advance—the Ten Commandments and

Sermon on the Mount notwithstanding. It is a demand of which one knows the precise meaning in the moment he is face-to-face with another person. No one needs to tell him then whether he is enabling another to step into his possibilities as a human being or has impeded the process. The experience is self-authenticating and he knows if he has chosen to be human or inhuman.

It is the refusal of God to conduct the affairs of men that creates the glory of man. And it is our decisions, moment by moment, that determine whether or not God is glorified in our lives.

12

The Other Kind of Hypocrite

I suspect that the most devastating thing one can say about a person is to label him a hypocrite. Few words evoke or express such strong feelings. No one likes the implication that there is any discrepancy between the way he is and the way he appears. To be charged with fraud at the core of one's being is threatening because it calls into question one's integrity.

Of course, there is a sense in which one cannot avoid pretense. One of the hardest things a child has to learn is that he cannot reveal every thought or express every feeling. In certain contexts he has to wear a mask. And that's what a hypocrite is, one who acts out a part. The sheer fact of the social order demands that we all be pretenders to some degree. It is neither possible nor desirable to be completely exposed. The very roles we accept cause us to alter our self-expression. Often with responsibility we change our patterns of behavior. Almost every person who accepts a public office becomes more virtuous as a leader than he ever was as a follower. And I suspect that we all make adjustments in our style to fit those in whose presence we find ourselves. We don't project quite the same image to someone we have just met as to someone whom we have known for a long time. A certain amount of pretending and concealing is as natural as it is inevitable.

But that's not hypocrisy in the more common use of the term. A hypocrite is one for whom pretending is a way of life. There is nothing steady or permanent in his personality, he seldom comes on straight, he consciously conceals the person he is and the values he holds. Few of us are that deceptive. Our hypocrisy is more occasional than fundamental. Certain persons and situations elicit it from us while others have no effect at all.

I

Perhaps we need to be reminded that there are really two kinds of hypocrites. Harry Kruener writes: "A hypocrite may be a person who pretends to be better than he really is, but a hypocrite may also be a person who pretends to be worse than he really is."[50] We most commonly think of a hypocrite as one who wants others to think better of him than he deserves. He will do almost anything to create a good impression. The classic illustration is the person whom we suspect appears at church to maintain his public image. His religious activities are a mask, a false front.

But the other kind of hypocrite may be more prevalent. If I had to identify the difference between this generation of youth and mine, I suspect one distinction might be at this point. While we erred in presenting ourselves as better than we were, this generation tends to project an image of being worse. Many of them go out of their way to create the impression that they are less interested in their studies, less attuned to moral values, and less socially responsible than they really are. Among peers in particular they undersell themselves. I'll always remember the description of one student by another. He reported that his roommate would say he was going to the Union when, in fact, he was bound for the library; he would talk about a course as if he were failing when, in fact, he was excelling; he would in class ask a dumb question when, in fact, he was capable of raising an insightful one. Many do not want to be known for the goodness they embody.

The Bible has little to say about this kind of hypocrite. It is usually concerned with the Pharisaical, those attentive to their public image of purity and piety. But I detect a reference to both kinds of hypocrisy in the parable of the prodigal son. You know the story. The prodigal approached his father for a share of his inheritance and when he had secured it took off for a far country where he lived it up. From the few hints in the narrative one can imagine the ingenuity with which he lived out every ignoble impulse. His elder brother played it safe and in staying home appeared to be a paragon of virtue. This son calculated his father's every expectation and falsified himself to meet it. He must have sneered in delight as others commended him for his good judgment. Yet underneath this pleasing posture lurked a rather uncompassionate and contriving spirit. The pose of goodness was cremated when the prodigal returned and was the recipient of his father's joy. With uncommon candor the older one protested that the father had lavished on the prodigal what was really due him. The elder brother was the kind of hypocrite who pretends to be better than he really is.

By contrast the prodigal pretended to be worse than he really was. He couldn't accept his essential goodness and live out the truth of his being. He had to wear the mask of a libertine to conceal the person he was. In the far country

"he squandered his property in loose living" (Luke 15:13).
Casting off every inner restraint and honest inclination, he
reduced himself to an object of contempt. In falsifying himself he disgraced his father's name, blurred every distinction between right and wrong, gave vent to every base
impulse. The prodigal was a hypocrite who was unable to
accept his goodness, so he projected every false image at
his command.

II

Of course, this raises the question of why we need to pre-
tend, why we present ourselves as better or worse than we
really are. The answer may be painful but it is not complex.
We are motivated by a fear that if others knew the truth
about us, they would reject us. Hypocrisy is a false search
for acceptance in which we are willing to compromise and
contradict our essential being to win approval. It is the
attempt to package ourselves in a marketable form, to cal-
culate what is demanded by our environment, then meet its
expectations. And, of course, the tragedy of it all is that this
seldom works—for long. In the interchange with others
we are more transparent than we realize. The trouble with
masks is that they never fit. It is obvious to everyone,
except sometimes ourselves, that we are out to falsify the
contours of our being. Few things are more futile than
pretense. Human beings may be very sophisticated and
ingenious in most areas of life, but we make rather poor
fakes. Let's be honest about that.

I have been contending that we are all hypocrites at times
and that this reveals an unwillingness to accept ourselves.
But how do we break the habit? How do we restrain the
impulse to pretense? I suspect that one begins with a re-

solve to so fully accept himself that one is free to reveal himself. That may sound like a simple solution to a complex problem. No one can deny the inertia we possess in relation to ourselves and the pain involved in coming to terms with ourselves. But I have also come to believe that there is no substitute for making decisions about ourselves and that laziness not fate is the barrier. The battle with pretense is won only by those who decide who and what they are going to be in the presence of others. It is within our power to choose the claims of our environment or to choose the claims of our essential being. That was the issue before the prodigal son. While he had earlier resolved to live out a false image of himself, in the far country "he came to himself" (Luke 15:17), chose to be who he really was. He resolved both to face himself and to be himself. He took into his self-identity both his purity and his impurity, both his noblest dreams and his distorted motivations, both his possibilities and his limitations. In simplest terms he resolved, "I am going to be me and no one else."

But this decision about himself was made in a context. And that is the point of the parable. His decision to be spontaneous and unaffected was made in the face of a decision made about him by his father. In the depths of his consciousness, the prodigal knew that there was one who could do no other than wait for him and rejoice in his return home. There was a father who knew all about him yet to whom the best and the worst made no difference in the intensity of his love. That was confirmed as the prodigal made his way into the sight of his father. "While he was yet at a distance, his father saw him and had compassion, and ran and embraced and kissed him." (Luke 15:20.)

Ultimately that is where the possibility of choosing to be oneself resides, where one finds himself freed of the need to keep up appearances. The word of life to the hypocrisy present in each is just this: There is One who knows more about us than we know about ourselves, whose love we cannot outdistance, and whose grace we cannot earn. We need not ask his name, the name may come later; we need not struggle to understand why, that can never be grasped; we need not defend it to others, only if they have experienced it will they understand; we need not ask for more, it is sufficient to our every need. All we can do is live each day in the assurance that this is the way life is. The utterly natural man is one who has made peace with that reality and experiences the joy of being the person he really is.

PART THREE
"TO DISCOVER HOW TO BE LOVING NOW"

13

The Moral Superiority of This Generation

Harvey Cox writes that "the current generation of college students and young adults . . . is neither devout nor deviant."[51] Many of their elders are not so sure. Most would agree that they are not devout in the traditional sense. Dispute centers upon their behavior and what, if anything, guides it. Some claim that the conscience of this generation has been anesthetized. Bishop Gerald Kennedy protests, "In my day they did it but they knew it was wrong." It disturbs him that the moral fences revered in his youth have been challenged. Perhaps it would be more accurate to say that this generation is not responsive to authority. It does not feel bound by tradition, it is suspicious of what is packaged in systems, and it distrusts everything that is established. By many of its elders this can only be interpreted as moral entrophy.

While most of us cannot suspect the worst of our own progenies, it has occurred to us that our law partner's son is a case in point. There must be something wrong with the values of a young man who lets his hair grow, bares his feet in public, and can make a Brooks Brothers suit look as though it had spent a decade on the Bowery. The most obvious sign of degeneracy is his manners—in response to the graciousness of his parents' friends he puts his hands in his jeans and grunts condescendingly. The causes he defends prove his poor judgment; one suspects he has taken an overdose of some college professor who never had to make a living in the real world. Thus the question for many vexed and perplexed elders is this: Whatever happened to that clean-cut and morally upright American youth who was the hope of the world?

Of course, there is a chance that we are talking about the wrong generation. *The Wall Street Journal* reported a revealing incident sometime ago. One father called another to protest that the latter's son repeatedly stole his son's pencils. The father pontificated at length about how important it was to teach children right from wrong at an early age. Then he added: "You understand it's the principle with which I am concerned, not the cost of the pencils. I can get all the pencils we need from the office." That may be a parable. And it interprets why this generation is cynical about the standards to which it has been exposed. Hypocrisy and duplicity are trademarks of the society that judges them and is immune to its own decadence. Those good old-fashioned moral verities and those venerable institutions give little evidence of moral sensitivity in response to the crucial issues of our time. This generation does not understand why white America can be so indignant over riots and so indifferent to the conditions that produced them. It does not understand why we sanction social and economic conditions in which the most expendable commodity is human beings. It does not understand the moral myopia of a governor who would bomb a nation back into the stone age and a mayor who instructs police to protect property before life. It does not understand a church that teaches morality and is silent on the crucial social issues of our time. If the authority of tradition and standards has been eroded, it may be because the tradition and standards are insensitive to the dynamics of our age.

I am prepared to argue for the moral superiority of this generation. It functions with an ethical sensitivity that puts my generation to shame. The wholesale rejection of our standards makes that difficult to grasp. But there is a moral compass functioning in their lives. It points in many of the same directions as our morality, but it responds to a different magnetic force.

I

The most obvious thing to be said about this compass is that it relies more upon imagination than regulation. Many of us accredit ourselves as moral persons by accepting the inherited wisdom of the ages. The Ten Commandments and the Sermon on the Mount chart our course; we live up to them as best we can. We know in advance what we ought to do, if not what we will do. Now for this generation that is a shortcut which protects one from the full burden of moral discrimination. It subverts rigorous scrutiny of the nuances in any given moment and the range of alternatives that may be open to him. The truly moral person travels light; that is the measure of his integrity. He will not dilute the awesomeness of his responsibility by relying on a regulation. That preempts agonizing appraisal of what would be moral and skips over to whether or not he will do it. It may be helpful to make a distinction between being disciplined and being sensitive. The disciplined person struggles to live up to his principles. Noble as that sounds, it may involve what Mark Twain called being a good man in the worst sense of the word. I suspect he was condemning that discipline by regulation which makes discrimination obsolete. This generation accents sensitivity as an alternative. What matters is to absorb the uniqueness of the moment and in that moment create a moral response. One would not presume to know in advance what is right, because one cannot know in advance the dynamics of the situation. To travel light morally is strenuous because it requires the use of our imagination.

It is the genius of this generation to have rediscovered that ethics is more a matter of being accountable to oneself than to principles. They would agree with Paul Tillich[52] that morality is the self-affirmation of one's essential being, it's an acting out of the intentionality of one's selfhood. In every moment I am choosing who I am going to be, not what I am going to obey. And one has to have the courage to live each moment with all the alternatives before him, trusting his own imagination as a means of improvising honor in the moment. On many college campuses students are agitating for self-determination of their social restrictions as opposed to the traditional regulations imposed by the faculty. Many respond by saying that they are normless and want more freedom to transform into chaos. But their revolt against standards is on behalf of a fuller understanding of responsibility. They want to make a decision and not accept a conclusion. Sometimes a person has to set principles aside in order to know what is right, even when he himself is doing it. I was intrigued recently by a study of student values and behaviors conducted at a large state university. One of the findings illustrates my point. When the students were asked if they counted virginity important as a standard, 89 percent said no. But when they were asked to register the extent of their sexual activity, the

results were no different from other generations who professed that virginity was crucial. There is rejection of a
standard and appropriation of its meaning. The moral
superiority of this generation is evident in their courage to
improvise in the moment what the integrity of their being
requires.

II

Some protest that the revolt against standards leaves this
generation without a moral authority. What these people
fail to understand is that there is a norm which guides their
moral compass. Harvey Cox argues that the people of this
generation have rediscovered experience, their own experience, as a cradle within which a norm is formed. And that
norm is not a set of principles passed down in all its pristine
purity. It is their understanding of what it means to be a
human being and what it is like to be destroyed as a person.
Indeed, they live in a world where this issue is drawn so
dramatically that they cannot understand the relevance of
any other norm. They struggle to make decisions that
enable themselves and others to be more fully human. This
generation would agree again with Paul Tillich that the
only moral imperative is to be "a person within a community of persons."[53] Their commitment is not to a system
but to a way of being. In every moment they are working
toward a style that sustains trust between persons, that
builds confidence in one another's richest possibilities, that
reaches for the most they can mean to one another. Words
like "hurt" and "pain" mean more than "evil" and "wrong."
The aversion to hurt and pain reflect their determination
not to destroy but to let one another "be." And the "letting
be" of ourselves and one another is the highest form of

morality. Those of us who dissent need to be reminded
that a relational imperative is more demanding than a regu-
lational one. A person can deceive the law but not the
haunting demands of love.

The people of this generation are not afraid of themselves. They trust their impulses, inclinations, and inten-
tions. My generation was attracted to Reinhold Niebuhr's
emphasis on the capacity of the self to deceive itself. No
one can fault that save for the fact that it is a half-truth.
Man is capable of spontaneous and uncalculated goodness
as well. There is a tremendous reservoir of integrity on
which we can rely in the moment of decision. One might
call the norm of this generation "the humane heart." That
is not an emotion, nor is it a sentiment; certainly it is not a
system. It is a disposition of one's whole being to be human
and to act for the humanizing of others. In the Bible the
heart is the county seat from which the politics of one's
being are legislated. It is the center of a man's selfhood
from which he thinks, feels, reflects, and ultimately acts.
It is where his humanness exists with hi-fi sensitivities and
psychedelic imagination. The humane heart can find in
each moment the uniquely relevant moral response. This
confidence the psalmist called "truth in the inward being"
(Ps. 51:6); it is what he coveted with the plea, "Teach me
wisdom in my secret heart." This is what the Holy One of
Israel demands—and it is the moral superiority of this
generation to have experienced the humane heart as a norm
and had the courage and imagination to live by it.

14

Words Are Events

We are apt to perceive words as no more than sounds or signs by which we communicate. They are that, to be sure; but they are much more. Words spoken and heard are formative events in our lives. When someone special says to you, "I love you," it does something to your relationship. If another whom you respect speaks a derogatory word, it does something to how you feel about yourself. When the doctor says, "You may have cancer," and then after an operation, "You do not have cancer," something happens to your life. The ancient Hebrews understood this implicitly. Their language has a symbol, *dabar,* which translates into English as "word" and means "event" as well. A word is both a sound and an event. Its effects are as real as something physical. Let's look more closely at what happens in this common process of speaking words to one another.

I

For one thing, each of us in large measure is defined by the words spoken to us. There is a direct relationship between who we are and what we hear. Obviously not all words have the same impact. Who says them and under what circumstances makes a difference. But that does not alter the fact that certain words have shaped the depths of our being, defined the contours of our personalities, and affected the very style of our lives. I'm sure you can cull from your memories moments when something was said to you that created a dimension of the person you are right now. I recall being caught in the second grade in the act of kissing the little blonde sitting in front of me. Knowing that the teacher would make good on her threat to report this act of sexual violence to my parents, I awaited their words with great apprehension. When I was invited to meet my father in the basement, I knew that the day of judgment had arrived. As he sat down in a wicker rocker and positioned his knees, I had a fair idea where the action was to be. Instead, he whisked me into his arms, rocked for a few moments, and then said: "Son, I just want to say one thing to you. When you kiss a woman it ought to mean something." That was all. But those words were an event which did much to define the man I would be in the presence of a woman.

It may seem unlikely that words can have that significant an impact; the frequency with which we hear them may lead us to underestimate their potency. But let me hold up a rather crude experiment conducted in the thirteenth century by Emperor Frederick, who ruled the Holy Roman Empire.[54] For some reason he wanted to know what was man's original language. Would Hebrew, Greek, or Latin come naturally to the lips of a child? He reasoned that if he isolated infants at birth from any human voices, they would eventually speak in the tongue natural to man. Frederick arranged for the infants to be reared by wet nurses, who were instructed to maintain silence in their presence. Difficult as it was for the women to restrain their inclination to speak to the infants, they complied with the order. The infants never heard a word. Within several months they were all dead.

The story points up that both our existence and our sanity "depend upon our being continuously and variably spoken to by those around us."[55] We are formed and deformed as persons by the words we hear. Jesus must have had this in mind when he interpreted the commandment, "Thou shalt not kill" (Ex. 20:13) to cover words spoken in anger. Whoever says, "Thou fool" (Matt. 5:22) kills as well. A verbal blow can be as lethal to the personality as a physical blow to the body. A man is the words spoken to him, and in every moment you and I are involved in the process of another's finding life or losing it. We ought not be afraid to speak; but we ought not speak without remembering that our words are events.

II

Recognizing that who we are is a function of the words we hear, we can also argue that the words we speak reveal what we have become. They are always to some degree an externalization of our being. We extend the truth about ourselves verbally into the lives of others. A person gives himself away in and through his words. Of course, some might counter that we use words to camouflage our real thoughts and feelings. We all know how that works. When feeling empty or anxious, we talk as if we did not have a care in the world; when without enough of significance to do, we talk about how busy we are. Yet, here and there other words escape our grasp and tell the truth about us.

Even in this moment as you read my words, I may be telling you more about myself than I care to! The persons we are inevitably leak out through the words we speak. In the final analysis, we are our words. Jesus put that rather bluntly when he said, "By your words you will be condemned" (Matt. 12:37). What we are is of a piece with what we verbalize.

Several years ago a group of psychologists in Boston decided to study juvenile delinquency and set up a rather interesting experiment. They employed a control group of delinquents to talk about themselves into a tape recorder. The assumption was that their words would constitute a trail by which the psychologists could unwind the dynamics of their personalities. In time, curiosity got the better of the delinquents and they asked to hear the tapes played back. When the experiment was over, they begged to go on with the process of speaking and then hearing themselves. While the psychologists were surprised, they should not have been; the request was a verification of their premise. The delinquents were coming to know themselves through listening to their own words.

Of course, there is an ancient maxim that actions speak louder than words. There may be some truth to that, but the distinction is a false one, for words are events in which the depths of our being are revealed. We stand exposed to ourselves by listening to ourselves. One of the things most of us do when we have a problem is to go talk to someone we trust. If that person is really helpful, he does not tell us what he thinks but what he has heard us say. As we hear him reflect back to us our own verbalizing, we see through our words into ourselves. And it is common for us to respond by saying, "You have told me something about myself I did not know." But that is not what has really happened. He has simply held our own words up to us until we saw ourselves in them. We are our words. The wise man listens to himself talking and along the way he comes to understand who he is.

III

I have been saying that words are events in which we are defined as persons and in which we are revealed as well. But there is a third dimension to our life in words. It focuses on the claim that God speaks. You can open the Bible to almost any book and come across the refrain, "And the word of the Lord came to a certain person saying . . ." I have always found that disturbing. It creates the image of someone who has learned how to dial heaven. Some believe that. When Billy Graham was confronted by the assertion that God is dead, he responded: "He can't be dead. I was just talking with him last night."

The implication that there is a supersensory apparatus through which God and man communicate is a distortion. God's address to us is embedded in our discourse with one another; it is the depth dimension of our verbal interaction. The Word of God is not in addition to but in, with, and under the words we address to one another. The only divine word we will ever hear is encapsulated in a human word.

Let me be more specific about what I mean. You are talking with a person, perhaps superficially, and word by word you find yourselves being drawn deeper into each other's lives. The roles and masks begin to slip away and you stand before each other fully and defenselessly. Your nearness is frightening but you know that what is happening is so real you don't care. And breaking through your listening and hearing, there is a Word from the Lord: "Love one another" (John 15:17). At another moment you may be interacting with a person whom you have offended deeply. The break in your relationship may seem beyond repair. The hostility is so high that reason is ineffective and reunion unthinkable. But then your words to each other begin to share the hurt and the shame of it all. Mutual trust and respect begin to take over and you accept each other in spite of what was between you. Then there is a Word from the Lord: "Forgive one another" (Eph. 4:32). Or perhaps you are sharing with another person the despair and emptiness that has been engulfing you. You may be thinking that if this is what life is like, you don't want any more of it. Yet as you talk it over, the clouds begin to recede, you can see ahead, the future begins to open up as having possibilities. Then there is a Word from the Lord between your words: "Abound in hope" (Rom. 15:13). Take one more situation. Someone may be representing before an audience of which you are a member the needs of others in this world. It may be the oppression of the Negro, the poverty of Appalachia, the illiteracy in the Orient, the need for technology in Latin America. As you listen to his words, you hear a claim upon you to alleviate these deprivations. Then there is a Word from the Lord: "Bear one another's burdens" (Gal. 6:2).

Do not be concerned about whether or not you can call the voice from the depths a Word from the Lord. It will be whatever it is regardless of your ability to name it. What is important is that you live by what you hear. The words of life come to us in every moment. Be doers of these words, not hearers only.

15
The Mask of God

Usually we think of David as the Biblical equivalent of a folk singer, as the lover of Bathsheba, or perhaps as the triumphant warrior; yet he is as well a father, a role he wrenches at times into hideous proportions. The most sordid descriptions of family life in popular journals pale before events in the royal household. As if in imitation of his father's lust, a son rapes his half sister. Their brother, Absalom, defends his sister's honor by slaying the offender. David said nothing about the rape; perhaps he couldn't. But he responded to the murder by expelling Absalom from his household. While the king is prevailed upon to lift the banishment, he decrees that the son is never to enter his presence. In the time of isolation from his father, Absalom plots the seizure of the throne for himself. Soon the armies of the father and the son are conjoined in battle. David's parting directive to his general is that the son be spared; a tinge of affection remains. Victory comes to the king, his reign over Israel is assured. But the joy of that is tempered with concern for Absalom. "Is it well with the young man . . . ?" (II Sam. 18:29.) David asks of a messenger from the front line. It is not; Absalom is dead. The dispirited David retreats to his chamber weeping: "O my son Absalom, my son, my son Absalom! Would I had died instead of you, O Absalom, my son, my son!" (II Sam. 18:33). While this event is not especially ennobling, it does raise the right questions, and I propose to use it as an aperture into the meaning of family life.

I

The first thing to be said is that the home is a place of both intimacy and distance. Our need for relationships in which a warm human presence is assured, where we can present ourselves to one another in all our strengths and weaknesses, is readily acknowledged. The intensity with which young people away at college anticipate vacations is at least in part explained by the desire to be where they are known and loved. But that this is as well a place of distance needs explanation. David's relationship with Absalom is enough to make us suspicious. Here was a father and a son who had only distance between them. For two years they existed in the same household without entering each other's presence. Out of that alienation came the revolt that ended in Absalom's death. This ought to suggest that distance is demonic.

The distortion, however, is not the distance, but its divorce from intimacy. Whenever David came close to his son it was a suffocating experience. In his household this overbearing king could only tolerate the shadow of a person. The son was forced to evaporate before his father. The distance of which we speak is a form of intimacy, the willingness to allow another to breathe the distinctiveness of his own existence. If we explore with caution the family life of Jesus, we see the struggle for that. When his mother and brothers became embarrassed by his ministry and sought to withdraw him from circulation, he responded with a rebuke: "Who is my mother, and who are my brothers?" (Matt. 12:48). Again at the wedding in Cana his mother asked him for a miracle to relieve the embarrassment of a host whose supply of wine was drained. He pushed her away from him, saying, "O woman, what have you to do with me?" (John 2:4). The very Christ who in the midst of his agony on the cross entrusted his mother to the care of his disciples was driven at times to demand distance, to struggle for separateness.

I became aware of that need in one of my daughters several years ago when she was four. I had been bearing down rather forcefully to conform her behavior to my expectations. Suddenly she looked up at me, a full four feet taller, and said, "You fink!" With dismay and anger I looked down at what I then perceived as my wife's daughter and asked, "What did you say?" With increased determination she pointed her little finger at me again and said, "You rat fink!" The teen-age baby-sitter who taught her those words is no longer in our employ! But I think I understand what she was saying: "Give me a little room of my own, I need to be a separate person."

When we gain some distance from one another, we may experience some delightful surprises. Offspring may discover in their parents talents and possibilities never before observed, a willingness to tolerate and encourage ideas foreign to their own, an eagerness to support us in plans not of their choosing. And parents may discover in their sons and daughters a quality of mind lacking in themselves, a vision of the future at once refreshing and exciting, aspirations and ideals in which they can only rejoice. When we meet as strangers in the home, we come away with a closeness never before experienced.

II

The second thing to be said about family life is that it is the place where love is shockingly indiscriminate. Here love does not affix itself because the object of affection is lovable or attractive. It claims the other person in the face of all that is unlovable and unattractive. Once again this is the tragic flaw in the David-Absalom relationship. They cut each other off when something did not suit their pleasure. David's response to his son's defense of his sister's honor was expulsion from his presence. And Absalom's response was to plot his father's defeat as king. For them love was conditional, dependent on the other's conforming to his expectations at the moment.

In the thirteenth chapter of I Corinthians, Paul describes a quality of love that is unconditional. Indirectly at least he is speaking of love within the family; some say explicitly. Listen to these familiar words through your own experience in the home. "Love is patient and kind; love is not jealous or boastful; it is not arrogant or rude. Love does not insist on its own way; it is not irritable or resentful; it does not rejoice at wrong but rejoices in the right. Love bears all things, believes all things, hopes all things, endures all things." (I Cor. 13:4–7.) This is love shockingly indiscriminate.

Late one afternoon in a Chicago suburb a teen-age gang was playing basketball in a backyard. Suddenly a dispute erupted over an alleged "foul." With profane expressions the youth whose yard it was dismissed the group from his property. Turning toward the house, he recognized his mother's face in the window; she had seen it all. He entered the kitchen knowing he was unlovable and expecting rejection. But the only words that fell upon his anxious ears were these: "Son, I have dinner ready for you, your favorite." He knew then that family love is shockingly indiscriminate, that one can be loved when he is unlovable.

In a popular novel of some years ago, one of the characters announces that "family life is only fit for those who can stand it."[56] And there are times when its demands and restrictions seem more than we can take. But where else can we stand if not in the place where nothing matters because of the way everything matters, where you cannot outdistance the care another has for you? It must have been just this the nineteenth-century theologian Friedrich Schleiermacher had in mind when he wrote his sister as his work was gaining recognition. Reflecting on the satisfaction of professional success, he wrote: "Nevertheless it would vanish from sight and I should count it as nothing compared to the prospect of a quiet, happy family life. . . . Except in family life all that we enjoy and all that we do in the world is vain and a deception."[57] With his theology he could only talk about shockingly indiscriminate love; in a home he could experience it.

III

Now there is a final word: the home is a place of sacramental relationships, where words and deeds are transparent to the depths of God. When intimacy is joined with distance, when love is shockingly indiscriminate, then the Eternal is present giving us a glimpse of the ultimate dimension to existence. Martin Luther spoke of family life as *larva Dei*, "the mask of God," a form in which his grace and goodness are revealed. God bundles himself in that human care which permeates family relations. When someone claims that for him God has become unreal and religion has lost its meaning, I always want to say a very simple word: "Go home, go where you are loved and the reality of God may return." You aren't likely to come up against him in reading theologians; you will never understand the depths of his graciousness in the quiet of the woods or before a setting sun; you probably will not be drawn to him through ancient creeds and curious confessions. His dwelling place is that human encounter where person bears with person the wonders of their existence. God is in and between relationships, mirrored one moment in a word, another in a deed.

You may be familiar with J. D. Salinger's continuing epic of the Glass family. In one episode, Franny has been sent home from college with an emotional disturbance that has taken the form of a search for a "holy man." She is obsessed with the saints, intrigued with religious personalities, repeats endlessly what she calls "the Jesus prayer." Her mother does not understand the strangeness in her daughter; all she can do is what she always has done when there was sickness in the family, retreat to the kitchen and brew her special chicken soup. The continual offer of it repels Franny; she wants religion. Finally her brother speaks a penetrating word: "If it's the religious life you want, you ought to know right now that you are missing out on every single goddam religious action that's going on around this house. You don't even have enough sense to *drink* when someone brings you a consecrated bowl of chicken soup."[58]

The ultimate incarnation of God is in his Son, but the immediate form his love for us may take is something as insignificant as a bowl of soup made sacramental in relationship. On that count, there is even a dimension of David transparent to the heart of God. With two sons dead, a daughter raped, family life destroyed, grace makes bold its presence as in brokenness he weeps: "O my son Absalom, my son, my son Absalom! Would I had died instead of you, O Absalom, my son, my son!" (II Sam. 18:33). Peering through that scene is the God whose love took death's form on a cross and in the sacrifice of himself gave life again to us.

The mask of God on calvary is born again in family life as persons risk themselves for one another. We shall forever have to look into the face of Jesus Christ to perceive the heart of God, but when we look away we may see it reflected for us in a mother or a father, yes, and in a son or a daughter.

16

The Courage to Accuse

The act of judging others creates some tensions for most of us in that we find ourselves at the mercy of two themes. One is the recognition that we have no right to condemn critically. Awareness of our own imperfections limits our inclination to make others aware of theirs. We don't see ourselves as fit to force our values upon those about us. "Who am I," we say, "to be another's judge?" Yet a second theme disrupts restraint: judgments are inescapable. Calculated and implicit evaluations mark almost every moment of life. Unworthy though we may be, the fact remains that we must discriminate. If it is not a colleague to be promoted or a person to be employed, it is a friend to be trusted or a ballot to be cast. Neutrality is seldom an option. Thus the dilemma in which we find ourselves is defined by the feeling that we have no right to judge others and the realization that we cannot escape it.

I

The first thing we need to understand about ourselves is that judging is always in some degree an "avoidance mechanism." We hasten to accuse others in order to avoid condemnation ourselves. With a rhetorical question Jesus identified this in the Sermon on the Mount: "Why do you see the speck that is in your brother's eye, but do not notice the log that is in your own eye?" (Matt. 7:3). The answer is implicit in the question. As long as we can draw attention to the defects in others, we prevent them from focusing upon ours.

I suspect this is why we thrive on gossip and slander. In itself there is nothing particularly interesting about someone's imperfections—in fact, they're about as boring as his ailments. But the satisfaction comes in escaping ourselves. As long as I can talk about another's morals, I do not have to think about my own. As long as I can concentrate on another's unpopularity, I do not have to acknowledge my own. As long as I can dwell upon the behavior of those around me, I call off discussion of my own. The censorious habit of mind that feeds on the defects of others is always a crude attempt to cover up our own.

But the irony of it is that there is nothing that gives us away as surely as what we select for condemnation in others. Jesus said, "With the judgment you pronounce you will be judged" (Matt. 7:2). Our accusations in at least some degree disclose the truth about ourselves. When lecturing to his students on that text, Martin Luther made this simple observation: "If I see something in . . . [another] that does not please me very much, I should draw back and take a look at myself."[59] Some of the most significant clues we ever get about ourselves are our reactions to those about us. We usually think of what a man stands for as most revealing of his character; but what he stands against in others may be more revealing of his true self. Judgments lay bare a man's soul as forcefully as convic-

tions. One of my colleagues has a stock reply to persons
who are obsessed with the morality of students: "I'm more
concerned with the morality of those who are concerned
with the morality of this generation." That may be a clever
evasion of the issue, but it also identifies what is involved
in judging others. What we seek out for censorship may
say more about us than about them. The judging of another is always a judgment of ourselves. "With the judgment you pronounce you will be judged." (Matt. 7:2.)

II

But this warning does not sanction moral indifference;
we need not be crippled by the risks we take in judging
others. In fact, the Biblical tradition nourishes the courage
to accuse. Perhaps the most conspicuous illustration is the
confrontation between King David and the prophet Nathan.
You may recall that David was attracted to Bathsheba and
satisfied his lust with her. When circumstances made the
reality of her husband an embarrassment, the king sent
Uriah into battle at a point where he was sure to be killed.
He used the power of his office to take possession of another's wife. When Nathan heard of this, he went to the
king with a parable. In a certain city, he said, there was
a rich man with many sheep and a poor man with one
lamb. A stranger came into their midst and asked food of
the rich man, who responded by slaughtering the poor
man's lamb. Upon hearing this, David was enraged: "As
the Lord lives, the man who has done this deserves to die"
(II Sam. 12:5,7). Nathan turned to his king and said,
"You are the man." You who have many wives have
taken the wife of Uriah who has one. Even knowing he
was imperfect, Nathan had the courage to accuse.

I detect in myself and in others a curious phenomenon. In one context we are willing to judge others with devastating ardor. We are willing to make substantial judgments based upon propriety; if there is a person in our community who deviates from the norms of the majority, we categorically dismiss him as a human being with feelings and possibilities. We are willing to make sweeping judgments based upon group identity; if a person is of a certain race or creed, our stereotypes can dismiss him without recourse to his uniqueness. Or we are willing to make sweeping evaluations of competence; if a doctor does not tell us what we need to hear, we write him off as a quack.

But while we are able to dismiss others, we usually are not willing to confront them. I don't like to admit this about myself or suggest it about others, but there are few with the courage to accuse directly. We settle for malicious gossip rather than attempt to help or heal. When it comes to sharing our feelings directly, we hide behind the old chestnut, "Who am I to judge another?" While bold behind their backs, we are cowards face-to-face. At this point we are moral pygmies. When our every feeling and conviction about honorable, responsible behavior has been violated, we lack the courage and integrity to accuse. When was the last time you risked telling even your best friend that his behavior or attitude offended you? Most of us silently simmer inside. And in keeping quiet we prostitute ourselves and deprive him of honest response.

III

We have been saying that, on the one hand, judging others is a revealing thing: we condemn ourselves in our judgments; and, on the other hand, that we need the cour-

age to accuse: it is the better part of honor to confront another directly. But now we need to ask: Who has the right
to accuse? Who is privileged to put himself against his
neighbor? Certainly not those who conceive of themselves
as morally pure, their self-righteousness disqualifies them;
certainly not those obsessed with their own unworthiness,
they cannot even accept themselves; the right to accuse
falls simply to those who perceive their neighbor to be
their responsibility, who feel accountable not only for
themselves but for all with whom they are gathered in the
bundle of life. Each of us must consider his neighbor and
think what is for his good and will build up the common
life.

That may sound too simple for some and too pious for
others. But it is the heart of what it means to be a Christian. To be in the form of Christ is to care deeply and pas-
sionately for one another, to see ourselves as commissioned
to bear with one another in the joys and burdens of life.
When the Catholic philosopher Baron von Hügel was on
his deathbed, he called to his side a niece who had been
his favorite. She bent her ear to his lips to hear his last
words. With the life that was left in him he shared the
thought that had ruled his life: "Caring is everything. Nothing matters but caring." Our mission in life, whatever else
we may do, is to care for one another, to risk identifying
with the triumphs and the tragedies of those around us.
The heights and the depths of our humanity are expressed
whenever we allow ourselves to get underneath the life of
another and share what he experiences. We'll never be a
whole person until we have risked standing alongside a
neighbor in his need.

For the most part we are a healthy and happy people.
But all of us have moments in which we cannot carry on

alone. There are some who feel condemned to suffer in solitude a secret pain; there are others intensely anxious about their ability to meet the tasks before them; there are some wounded by a love not reciprocated and feel rejection at the depths of their being; there are others perplexed by moral dilemmas beyond their strength to resolve; and there are some burdened by what they will do with their lives beyond the year at hand. All about us is a world of hurts and woundings that cry out for the healing presence of another person who cares.

If you set yourself to the task of responding to others as your strength permits, of being available and willing to bear the burdens they may set upon you, you will know some of the deepest joys and satisfactions in life. And in the midst of your caring, you will someday come to know One who cares for you, the God whose presence is known in the ordinary commerce between human beings. The nearer you come to your neighbor, the nearer you will be to the God who cares for both of you, even to a cross. He is revealed to human beings who share one another's lives as if they were their own.

The point of it all is this: we have the right to accuse our neighbor to the extent we care for him. In fact, our accusations will reveal how deeply we care.

17

The Sacred Sense of Touch

It is not often that one's FOURTH CLASS MAIL is enticing! But when the Greek word for lusty love is boldly printed in one corner of the envelope and "Intellectuals, Unite" across the foot, what insecure professor can resist a glance inside? On the letterhead was a picture of Marilyn Monroe making a feeble attempt to compensate with her hands for the absence of clothing. The reader is informed that before her death Miss Monroe exposed herself to a photographer and that a subscription to a certain magazine will bring twenty-four pages of her fleshy expanse. The claim is not particularly shocking that this will be "the rave of the American Intellectual Community." One assumes that this is a polite reference to the college boys in their fraternity houses! The shock of recognition comes when the editor says he knows you are the type of person who would be interested. For the moment one forgets that this is a bulk mailing and is haunted by the question, "How did he find out?"

The perversion in the propaganda, however, is the assumption that sex can be isolated from one's selfhood, observed for aesthetic and intellectual growth. It is presented as having a sovereign domain of its own without reference to love and one's essential humanity. To this extent it reflects a cultural perception that takes many forms. In *Playboy,* sex is treated as purely recreational; in the Kinsey reports, as exclusively biological; and in jokes, as a thing about which one jests as a symbol of liberation. Thus perceived, it is nothing but a distortion.

It will neither further nor deepen our understanding to examine the most recent studies of sexual behavior. Vance Packard in *The Sexual Wilderness* argues that the behavior of college women is evidence of a change in sexual mores. But even if his study is reliable, it provides no insight into our own sexuality. To assault the drives within us or others with the weaponry of moralisms is to lose before one starts. Prohibititions and inhibitions lost their grip some decades ago—or was it in the Garden of Eden? Yet there is an alternative to statistical calculation and moralistic manipulation. Decisions in the realm of sexuality can be made with reference to the sacred sense of touch. That is the Biblical clue. Scripture may have its share of regulations, but at core it has a dynamic understanding of what goes on when we make physical contact with another person. That is the most flexible and demanding context within which our decisions about behavior can be made.

I

The first thing that must possess our understanding is that sex is a function of the whole person. It is not something you do with your body alone; your total being as a person is involved. Man is not created a loose composite of parts operating independently of one another. We are an "embodied spirit" and sex is a function of our selfhood. All we are as persons is drawn up into what we do with our bodies. The "you" can never be withdrawn from the body thus freeing it to indulge itself indiscriminately.

This is difficult to discern from the Biblical tradition rendered in English. Whenever we come across the word "body" we assume the reference is to our physical nature. Behind these translations, however, is the Hebrew word *nephesh,* which literally means a union of body and spirit, and the Greek word *soma,* which means the total person, all that is you. Any part of us is an extension of all of us. Thus the strange command of Jesus takes on meaning: "If your hand or your foot causes you to sin, cut it off; . . . if your eye causes you to sin, pluck it out" (Matt. 18:8–9). This is not an exhortation to mutilation but a perception of our nature. All of me is involved in what my hand, foot, or eye does. A physical act is a function of the whole personality.

In Alan Paton's novel *Too Late the Phalarope,* there is a profoundly Biblical insight into this essential unity. A young Afrikander and his wife are devout Protestants, but she is unable to love him in any complete physical way. She polarizes with the spirit as good and the body as evil. Attempting to communicate the meaning of sexuality to her, Pieter says: "It's all together, the body and mind and soul, between a man and a woman. When you love me as you've done, I'm comforted in all of them. And when I love you as I've done, it's you I love, your body and mind and soul." Later in silent dialogue with himself he says, "And I wanted to cry out at her that I could not put the body apart from the soul, and that the comfort of her body was more than a thing to the flesh, but was a comfort of the soul . . . as well."[60]

This is the same understanding represented in the Biblical affirmation that two become "one flesh." There is a blending of total persons when they physically encounter one another. It is not two bodies but two personalities that come together in all the mystery of their being. Paul even goes so far as to say that "he who joins himself to a prostitute becomes one body with her" (I Cor. 6:16). Here of all places one might be inclined to see it in purely biological terms. But even in this distortion something happens to two persons. They literally exchange themselves with each other, even though it is outside the love and trust within which this mutual giving can have meaning.

II

This leads directly into a second dimension of human sexuality. Because it is an encounter of two persons, it is an act in which each comes to know himself and the other. An awareness of the mystery of one's own and the partner's being is crystallized. The most real things about ourselves are known and shared in the sex act. Each "I" needs a "Thou" up against which he comes to himself and in relation to whom he can give himself freely. When God looked upon Adam in the Garden of Eden he perceived his incompleteness and said, "It is not good that the man should be alone; I will make him a helper fit for him" (Gen. 2:18). I will make one with whom his life can come into fullness. The female is posited in creation because without her man is incomplete.

In this context it is significant that the Bible frequently uses the verb "to know" for sexual intercourse. Two persons really come to know themselves and each other in their physical encounters. The man discovers what it means to be a man in relationship to a woman, and the woman finds her own self in relationship to a man. Sex is the profound and mysterious capacity by which persons become themselves in all their individuality and share themselves in all their uniqueness.

In her novel *The Mandarins,* Simone de Beauvoir treats this in a glib and superficial way. In the course of the plot Nadine gives knockout drops to a man so that she may climb in bed with him. When Henri awakens and realizes what has happened, Nadine blithely explains: "I wanted to get to know you. . . . When you sleep with someone, it helps to break the ice."[61]

But it was never conceived for breaking the ice between strangers. It is an act in which we share the deepest secrets of our being. What we give is not primarily our needs and passions but ourselves. That is the noblest gift a man and woman have for each other. The touch of two bodies is sacred because it is the expression of their willingness to share their lives in all their splendor and agony. The secrets of one's own existence are simply too precious to be exposed indiscriminately. " 'All things are lawful for me,' " said Paul, "but not all things are helpful." (Cor. 6:12.)

Sex, then, is a form of communication between two persons; but it is always more. When self meets self both are met by the Ultimate Self, by the God who created them for each other. Sex always points beyond itself to the realization of two persons that they are fulfilling their essential nature before One who is essential to them both. Through the ages it has been perceived as a sacrament because it has the capacity to disclose the love of God. He is never more real in our lives than when two persons are real to each other. The man who loves a woman and whose life comes to fullness in hers eventually looks beyond their joy in each other to the God who is the love between them.

III

Because the sacred sense of touch is a disclosure of two persons to each other, it belongs in the context of commitment. In Françoise Sagan's novel *A Certain Smile,* one of her characters is asked what she means by love. She responds, "Love means thinking about a man, going out with him, liking him better than anyone else."[62] This matches our usual perception of it as a feeling of compatability and joy in another's presence. But it is more than that. Love is a giving and receiving controlled by a sense of responsibility, a commitment which takes into itself the task of affirming the unique and precious nature of the other. Don Juan is a weakling, not a hero, in the sphere of love because his commitment is only to his own distorted needs. He does not have the strength to seek and be faithful to the well-being of a woman. The recipient of his affections is no more than an object he exploits for his own gratification. True love is not a matter of being together but of belonging together and the contemporary Don Juans simply do not have the stuff for that. Sex is the most full giving of the self to another of which we are capable and unless two are bound by lifelong pledges of fidelity the mutual surrender is tepid and cheap.

When you come to the altar to be married the minister does not say, "Do you two feel you are in love?" He exacts a declaration of intent: "Wilt thou have this Man to be thy husband, and wilt thou pledge thy troth to him, in all love and honor, in all duty and service, in all faith and tenderness, to live with him, and cherish him, according to the ordinances of God, in the holy bond of marriage?" Feelings of love are never enough. They must embody the determination to be affirming and faithful: "In plenty and in want; In joy and in sorrow; In sickness and in health; As long as we both shall live." And it is significant that at the conclusion of the service the minister does not say, "I make you husband and wife." He merely announces to the congregation that they are husband and wife because of the "covenant between them made."[63]

Now the Biblical understanding of our sexuality is fraught with what Reinhold Niebuhr has called "impossible possibilities." None of us comes to it fully aware that it is an act of his total being; none of us ever cherishes sufficiently the mystery of his own self and that of the other; and none of us ever assumes full responsibility for the object of his love. But the Christian knows that the bond between a man and a woman does not depend upon their determination alone; it is guaranteed by the God who has created them for each other and whose goodness is reflected in their union. By his grace we are daily released from our perversities and freed for the sacred sense of touch.

18

The Search for a Viable Community

It has been contended that there are two dominant and ostensibly secular quests in our time.[64] One is the search for a personal style, a way of achieving a significant life as an individual. It is the quest for meaning as a unique person in a unique period of history. And the other search is for a political vision, a sustaining community through which one can effect the contours of our age. It is the quest for a communal form of impact upon one's environment. Implicit in both is a rejection of speculation about reality and conjectures about morality that intrigued previous generations. Contemporary man is curiously pragmatic. He is concerned to devise a personal style and a political vision that work. It is the search for a viable community that I choose now to explore.

Not much imagination is required to recognize that most existing structures are suffering a crisis of confidence and effectiveness. Those sustaining communities through which men have had an impact have generally lost their vision of the future and committed themselves to conservation of the past. The forces of consolidation in institutions with recognized authorities and legitimized goals have lost touch with the progressive elements of their constituencies. Several come to mind. Labor unions, once a revolutionary cadre which stood up to the industrial establishment, have themselves become a bastion of complacency. The 1968 political campaign is evidence that unions are no longer instruments of change but centers of resistance to it. The university as a corporate body is experiencing torturous divisions. One does not have to look far or search deeply to note the inability of faculty, students, and administrators to mobilize their resources toward common goals. One educator has argued that the disillusionment of students with the church led them to trust the university as a community for impact only to be more profoundly disillusioned. Then one might consider what is happening to our political parties. While in other times they were energized by a common ideology and a promise to enact it, now they are communities of convenience. Party loyalty tends to be irrelevant. Citizens increasingly vote across party lines because the issues divide that way.

Evidence abounds that traditional communities of impact lack cohesion and vision; no longer are they satisfying or advantageous. We desperately need sustaining communities with the wit and power to manage the future. The day at hand is ready for "a new grouping of men resolved to speak out clearly and pay up personally."[65] But before we rush to ask where we will find such a community we have to ask what it will be like if we do.

I

We need, first, a grouping of persons committed to the rhetoric of expectancy. With the recent assault upon spoken and written language by Marshall McLuhan, the extent to which language initiates reality has been obscured. At best we think of words as symbols that feebly reflect what already exists. They do that to be sure. Verbalization often is no more than after-the-fact reporting. But words also have the capacity to be agents of novelty and innovation. They bring into being what did not before exist. Several years ago the twentieth anniversary of the Battle of Britain was observed. At one celebration a Royal Air Force pilot was asked what had enabled him and his comrades to continue beyond all human endurance. He responded that the answer was contained in the speeches of Winston Churchill. He taught the English people "the language of courage." It did not exist before. "It was not until Churchill had 'taught' them this language that such courage became for them a possibility, and then a reality which made it possible for them also to be courageous."[66] Rhetoric is never the sole cause of whatever is, but there are times when it is the dominant constituting force of reality.

The rhetoric of expectancy assumes that the future is ours to manage. It verbalizes what we anticipate of the future and in the process begins to establish it. Perhaps the most compelling example is the political efforts of Senator Eugene McCarthy. I'm not sure that anyone in our time has the perspective to grasp fully the dynamics of his impact but one thing is clear: he was able to articulate the aspirations of many for the nation and give the sense that he was with his words creating a new reality. One had the feeling that he was both saying something and doing something. The Senator was in many ways an answer to the claim of Harvey Cox that we need "a rekindling of the capacity for political fantasy."[67] In part Cox was calling forth that function of dreamers and visionaries who can picture possibilities toward which a sustaining community can

move. But more than that he was calling for that rhetoric
of expectancy which creates realities with the act of speaking. Perhaps the motto of our time ought to be both "tell it
like it is" and "tell it like it ought to be." We need to talk
our dreams into reality and our delusions into oblivion.
That is what the prophets did rather consistently. Think of
Amos. Speaking to his people on behalf of God, he said:
"I hate, I despise your feasts, and I take no delight in your
solemn assemblies. . . . Take away from me the noise of
your songs; to the melody of your harps I will not listen."
That's telling it like it is. "But let justice roll down like
waters, and righteousness like an everflowing stream."
(*Amos* 5:21, 23–24.) That's telling it as it ought to be.
And with the rhetoric of expectancy he created a commu-
nity given to the fulfillment of his "political fantasy."

There can be little doubt of the need for a coalition of
men committed to managing the future. And I am convinced that it is with the rhetoric of expectancy they must
begin. Words reflect what has happened, but they also create what will happen.

II

Then we need, secondly, a grouping of men who are determined to "redesign human institutions."[68] It is self-evident that the machinery of our society no longer functions
in favor of the future. For the most part it conserves and
perpetuates the values and needs of the past. This is why
more radical movements have advocated the destruction of
existing institutional forms. It is difficult to forget the way
in which this came to expression at Berkeley through the
words of Mario Savio: "There is a time when the operation
of the machine becomes so odious, makes you so sick at
heart that you can't take part; you can't even tacitly take

part, and you've got to put your bodies on the levers, upon all the apparatus, and you've got to make it stop. And you've got to dictate to the people who own it, that unless you're free, the machine will be prevented from working at all." It is not difficult to imagine the frustration which has produced that program. The dominant institutions of our culture—government, industry, church, labor unions, universities—are geared to maintain the *status quo*. As presently constituted they have the power and public consensus to conserve the past rather than conceive the future. It is interesting how frequently the word "irrelevant" comes into play. The church is said to be irrelevant to the urban-technological culture; the university is irrelevant to the learning aspirations of students; the government is irrelevant to the real needs of the poor and oppressed.

But this very irrelevance at the centers of power is a challenge to our imaginations and ingenuity. As Harvey Cox writes, "The political mandate we face is not one of legitimizing stability but of facilitating orderly change."[69] Those who choose to have a constructive impact upon our time need to infiltrate the system and possess for their vision of the future the levers of change. And that takes more wisdom, courage, and political skill than bringing it to a screeching halt. It requires a willingness to bring upon oneself the hostility of those who benefit from the *status quo*. It demands the restraint to thwart the violence of indifference without creating the violence of revolution. It involves the political skill to outwit those who sit sanctimoniously in the positions of authority. It calls for a commitment to principles that neither aspires to personal gain nor is frustrated by personal discreditation. It is not easy to go where the action isn't and establish it without creating chaos but it's the most pressing task of our time. Martin Luther King, Jr., did it for the issue of race, Eugene

McCarthy did it for the issue of peace, and countless students are doing it for the issues of education.

But for what precisely must the institutions be redesigned? Toward what goal do we need to gear up the machinery? The answer is in the word "justice," properly understood. And as Daniel Day Williams writes, "We mean by justice an order of life which gives to each member of the community the fullest possible access to the sources of fulfillment."[70] That is not an abstract prescription but a concrete objective. It requires of us that we draw up into the centers of decision-making the fullest possible range of participation—whether it is in the ghetto or in the university. It means that we make available to all, regardless of their abilities or even their efforts, a minimal standard of living—whether we do it through the guaranteed annual wage or the negative income tax. It sets us to the task of assaulting any and all systems that institutionalize prejudice —whether it is the country club or the political machine which devours funds intended for education. It necessitates for many of us the death of old myths with all the pain and alienation that it entails and the birth of a new heart dedicated to compassion and conscience rather than expediency and privilege. Half a century ago William James said that what we need is the moral equivalent of war. And we have it now in the task of setting the institutions of our time to the cause of justice. Granting access to the sources of fulfillment to all members of the community is the common task for a grouping of men aspiring to an uncommon impact upon their age.

III

But there is an issue that now must be faced. Does the viable community for which we search with its discipline in the rhetoric of expectancy and its determination to redesign human institutions for justice—does it require the formation of a new body which does not now exist or is there a structure that can be set to that task? Ultimately I believe it is necessary to align ourselves with an existing institution lest we multiply the bureaucracy. And for me and others in our time the institution with the possibilities for this responsibility—well hidden in most instances—is the church. And I say that not because of any great enthusiasm for its present state but because of its historic commitment to and understanding of hope and justice. Sometime ago I had the opportunity to ask urban revolutionary Saul Alinsky why it was consistently people of the church who initiated, supported, and ultimately responded to his summons for revolution. I was not prepared for his answer, though, indeed, I should have been. "It is," he said, "in the Judeo-Christian tradition that one finds the metaphors and images for transformation. This people has within its corporate memory the archetypal symbols which express and respond to revolutionary action for justice."

For many of us the church is the natural base for the sustaining community through which we can have an impact upon our age. It is a Trojan horse already residing in the city of civilization. Within it are men who with Paul see themselves as "a colony of heaven" (Phil. 3:20, Moffatt translation), an outpost in this world for the God in whom we ultimately hope and in whom we commit ourselves to justice.

Notes

1. Paul Tillich, *Systematic Theology* (University of Chicago Press, 1951), Vol. I, p. 47.

2. W. H. Auden, "For the Time Being," in *Religious Drama/ 1:5 Plays*, Martin Halverson (ed.) (Living Age Books, Meridian Books, Inc., 1957), pp. 33–35.

3. Michael Novak, "Human First, Christian Second," *The Christian Century*, June 19, 1968, p. 815.

4. Albert Camus, *Resistance, Rebellion and Death* (London: Hamish Hamilton, Ltd., 1961), pp. 50–51.

5. Translated by John D. Godsey in "Reading Bonhoeffer in English Translation: Some Difficulties," *Union Seminary Quarterly Review,* Fall, 1967, p. 89.

6. Richard L. Rubenstein, *After Auschwitz* (The Bobbs-Merrill Company, Inc., 1966), p. 245.

7. Quoted in Kay M. Baxter, *Contemporary Theater and the Christian Faith* (Abingdon Press, 1964), p. 72.

8. Quoted by Gene E. Bartlett in a sermon preached at Colgate Rochester Divinity School.

9. Otto Butz (ed.), *To Make a Difference,* quoted in *Time,* June 9, 1967, p. 90.

10. Archibald MacLeish, *J.B.* (Houghton Mifflin Company, 1958), p. 153.

11. Schubert M. Ogden, *The Reality of God* (Harper & Row, Publishers, Inc., 1963), p. 37.

12. *Ibid.,* p. 37.

13. Quoted by Bernard C. Murchland in *Camus: A Collection of Critical Essays,* Germain Bree (ed.) (Prentice-Hall, Inc., 1962), p. 59.

14. From the review by Malcolm Muggeridge of *The Autobiography of Bertrand Russell 1914–1944* in *The Observer Review, London,* April 28, 1968.

15. Schubert M. Ogden, "How Does God Function in Human life?" in *The Credibility of "God",* a colloquium at Muskingum College, March 20–21, 1967, p. 33.

16. Fritz Buri, "How Can We Still Speak Responsibly of God?" *Andover Newton Quarterly,* November, 1967, p. 127.

17. Sidney M. Jourard, *Disclosing Man to Himself* (D. Van Nostrand Company, Inc., 1968), p. 223.

18. Ogden, *loc. cit.,* p. 16.

19. Charles Hartshorne, "God and the Social Structure of Reality" in *The Credibility of "God,"* p. 19.

20. Samuel H. Miller, *Man the Believer* (Abingdon Press, 1968), p. 38.

21. Edward Albee, *The Zoo Story* (Coward-McCann, Inc., 1960), p. 43.

22. Henry Miller quoted by Samuel H. Miller in "The Clown in Contemporary Art," *Theology Today,* October, 1967, p. 324.

23. Samuel H. Miller, *loc cit.,* p. 327.

24. Wolfgang M. Zucker, "The Clown as the Lord of Disorder," *Theology Today,* October, 1967, p. 309.

25. *Ibid.,* p. 308.

26. Samuel H. Miller, *loc. cit.,* p. 328.

27. Martin Luther, *Werke* (Weimarer Ausgabe, 1883), p. 483, quoted by Erik H. Erikson, *Young Man Luther* (W. W. Norton & Company, Inc., 1958), p. 241.

28. Paul Tillich, *Systematic Theology* (University of Chicago Press, 1951), Vol. I, p. 10.

29. Joseph Sittler, *The Ecology of Faith* (Muhlenberg Press, 1961), p. 69.

30. Quoted in Joseph Sittler, *ibid.,* p. 70.

31. Abraham J. Heschel, *God in Search of Man* (Farrar, Straus & Giroux, Inc., 1955), p. 57.

32. Quoted in Abraham J. Heschel, *ibid.,* p. 57.

33. *Ibid.,* p. 75.

34. Arthur Koestler, *Dialogue with Death* (The Macmillan Company, 1942), p. 120.

35. John Steinbeck, *Sweet Thursday* (Bantam Books, 1954), p. 96.

36. John A. T. Robinson, *Honest to God* (The Westminster Press, 1963), p. 99.

37. Harvey Cox, *The Secular City* (The Macmillan Company, 1965), p. 51.

38. *Ibid.,* p. 45.

39. *Ibid.,* p. 47.

40. Cornelis A. van Peursen, "Man and Reality—The History of Human Thought," *The Student World* (1st quarter, 1967), p. 13.

41. Quoted in Roger L. Shinn, *The Search for Identity: Essays on the American Character* (Harper & Row, Publishers, Inc., 1964), p. 190.

42. Eric Hoffer, "The Cult of Violence Loose in America," *The Columbus Dispatch,* July 27, 1968.

43. Martin Luther King, Jr., "I Have a Dream," reprinted by The Fellowship of Reconciliation in a pamphlet *Unwise and Untimely.*

44. *Ibid.*

45. Wyatt T. Walker, "Faith as Taking the Risk," *Theology Today,* July, 1968, p. 210.

46. Kyle Haselden, "Obscenity Beyond Sex," *The Pulpit,* November, 1967, p. 3.

47. *Webster's New International Dictionary* (2d ed., G. & C. Merriam Company, 1955), p. 1212.

48. Quoted by Robert H. Hamill in "Nobody Is a Nobody," a sermon preached at Boston University, February 19, 1967.

49. Viktor E. Frankl, *From Death-Camp to Existentialism* (Beacon Press, Inc., 1959), p. 65.

50. Harry H. Kruener, *Specifically to Youth* (Harper & Brothers, 1959), p. 70.

51. Harvey Cox (ed.), *The Situation Ethics Debate* (The Westminster Press, 1968), p. 11.

52. Paul Tillich, *Morality and Beyond* (Harper & Row, Publishers, Inc., 1963), pp. 20 ff.

53. *Ibid.*, p. 18.

54. Earl A. Loomis, Jr., *The Self in Pilgrimage* (Harper & Row, Publishers, Inc., 1960), p. 54.

55. *Ibid.*, p. 56.

56. Quoted by Robert Fitch in *The Decline and Fall of Sex* (Harcourt, Brace & World, Inc., 1957), p. 45.

57. Quoted by Richard R. Niebuhr, *Schleiermacher on Christ and Religion* (Charles Scribner's Sons, 1964), p. 22.

58. J. D. Salinger, *Franny and Zooey* (London: William Heinemann, Ltd., 1962), p. 194.

59. Jaroslov Pelikan, *Luther's Works* (Concordia Publishing House, 1956), Vol. 21, p. 215.

60. Alan Paton, *Too Late the Phalarope* (Charles Scribner's Sons, 1953), pp. 87–88.

61. Quoted by Robert Fitch, *op. cit.*, p. 12.

62. Françoise Sagan, *A Certain Smile* (E. P. Dutton & Co., Inc., 1956), p. 102.

63. *Marriage Service*, Board of Christian Education of The United Presbyterian Church in the U.S.A.

64. Harvey Cox, "The Secular Search for Religious Experience," *Theology Today*, October, 1968, pp. 321 ff.

65. Albert Camus, *Resistance, Rebellion and Death* (London: Hamish Hamilton, Ltd., 1960), pp. 50–51.

66. Paul J. Achtemeier, "How Adequate Is the New Hermeneutic?" *Theology Today*, April, 1966, p. 118.

67. Harvey Cox, *loc cit.*, p. 324.

68. John W. Gardner, unpublished speech at the American Council on Education, October 10, 1968.

69. Harvey Cox, *loc. cit.*, p. 323.

70. Daniel Day Williams, *The Spirit and the Forms of Love* (Harper & Row, Publishers, Inc., 1968), p. 250.